The Burgundian Wars

Detlef Ollesch and Hagen Seehase

Translation by Richard Sanders

"On this day we departed with six from our city against the Burgundian Duke, we had several groups before us that were strong in men and equipment"

"Wir sind diser tag gegen den Burguschen Hertzog uff Sechs mit von unser Statt gezogen, haben vor ettlich Stossen, die vast mit lüt und gezüg bestarkt gewesen sind"

(From a letter from the Bernese Council to the Council of Ulm after the Battle of Grandson, written in old Swiss dialect)

Authors' Acknowledgements

We owe our thanks to Stefan Mueller and the whole team at Zeughaus Verlag who made this book possible.
To Florian Messner for his advice and support – and translations from Italian – we are grateful.
We thank Thomas Vaucher for the foreword and identification of errors.
Christian Amet, Michael Gauger, Anja and Michael Hiebinger, Florian Messner, Susan Sümer, Thomas Vaucher, Marko Tjemmes and Marco Zanoli provided photos and illustrations.

Authors: Detlef Ollesch and Hagen Seehase
Maps: Bernhard Glänzer and Marco Zanoli
Translation: Richard L. Sanders

Publisher: Zeughaus Verlag GmbH
Knesebeckstr. 88
10623 Berlin, Germany

Telephone: +49 (0)30/315 700 30
Email: info@zeughausverlag.de
Website: www.zeughausverlag.de

All rights reserved.
Reproduction, translation and photographic reproduction, including extracts are forbidden. Storage and distribution including transfer onto electronic media like CD-ROM, etc., as well as storage on electronic media like the Internet, etc., are not permissible without the express written permission of the publisher and are punishable.
Bibliographic information from the Deutschen Bibliothek: The Deutsche Bibliothek lists this publication in the German National Bibliography; detailed bibliographic information is available at http://dnb.ddb.de.

Printed in European Union
Originally published in German as "Die Burgunderkriege"
in the Heere & Waffen series number 30 (Berlin: Zeughaus Verlag, 2018)
© 2019, 2024 ZEUGHAUS VERLAG GmbH, Berlin, Germany

ISBN: 978-3-96360-014-2

Contents

Foreword 9

The Duchy of Burgundy – the Dukes of Burgundy 11

The Siege of Neuss 16

Unrest in Alsace and the High Rhine[1] 22

Burgundian Domination on the Upper Rhine 25

The Uprising against Charles the Bold's Steward 30

The Swiss Confederation's First Attacks on Burgundy 36

Campaign of Conquest in Waadt (Vaud) 37

Description of the Storming of a Castle by Swiss Fighters 38

Secondary Theaters of War in Wallis (Valais) and Lothringen (Lorraine) .. 42

Description of a Deployment of a Swiss Contingent 47

The Battle of Grandson 48

The Battle of Murten/Morat 54

The Battle of Nancy 63

The Aftermath 68

The Armies and Weapons of the Burgundian Wars 70

    The Burgundian Army 70

    The Swiss and Their Allies 89

The "Hens' War" (Hennenkrieg) 98

Burgundian "Ordonnance" Companies 99

Bibliography 100

---

[1] The High Rhine (German: *Hochrhein*) is the name used for the part of the Rhine that flows westbound from Lake Constance to Basel

FOREWORD

The conflict between the apparently much more powerful Duke of Burgundy, Charles the Bold, and the small Swiss Confederation had always fascinated me as an ancestor of these seemingly courageous Swiss. Not dissimilar to the unyielding Gauls from "Asterix and Obelix" who defiantly stood up against the Roman Empire, the Swiss were also able to defy their mighty enemy.

From 2004 to 2010 when I wrote my first historical novel ("The Lion of Burgundy"[2]) precisely about this topic, I would have not thought Charles the Bold and his life would accompany me in the future. Thus a few years later the historical non-fiction book "The Engadine War[3]" came about in which I was able to make a contribution to this subject (and in which I also worked on Burgundian Wars from a historical perspective after the fiction version), and this was before I received a request from Hagen Seehase to write the foreword to this work.

When doing the extensive research for "The Lion of Burgundy", I would have been very happy about and thankful for a publication like this one. The many interesting details about weapons, armor and organization of the opposing armies would have clearly made my research easier. It's true there are "Men-at-Arms" volumes ("Armies of Medieval Burgundy" and "The Swiss at War") in English from Osprey Publishing, indeed one looks in vain for similar sources in German.

When I received the manuscript for this book, it led me to realize that I could also learn many interesting things that I could have used when writing my novel. For example, that Charles the Bold, to save money he owed in pay to his troops, had them fight in the foremost ranks or that the Burgundians produced smoke screens to protect themselves when attacking; that for a time there were 73 armorers in Brussels; that the large bombards used stone balls because the gas pressure that occurred with iron balls caused the barrels to explode; or that the mummified "pseudo-head of Peter von Hagenbach" is still kept in Colmar, just to give a few examples.

So, I hope that this book will ease the research of some readers interested in history to satisfy their thirst for information about Charles the Bold and his times or to inspire them about some interesting episode (like those mentioned above).

Thomas Vaucher
Giffers, Switzerland, June 2017

Authors' Preliminary Remarks

The events described in this book took place in a region that belongs in part to the German-speaking and in part to the French-language area.

The place names and persons' names are oriented on their cultural affiliation at the time of the events. Thus, for example, the place names in the Alsace are given in German (with the French name following after the first use, for example Mülhausen (Mulhouse)).

The Burgundian Duke Charles the Bold, however, who had a well-known role in history, is given in the usual way, not in the actually correct form of "Charles I le Téméraire".

Translator's Notes

Quotations in the medieval Swiss German language shown in the original German version of the work have been retained in that archaic language, but also translated into English whenever possible. The original Swiss German is generally provided in the footnotes.

When the term "Empire" is used, it refers to the Holy Roman Empire, located at the time in what is now Germany and Austria and some more far flung territories. The terms Kaiser and Emperor are used interchangeably, but both refer to the head of the Holy Roman Empire. Where Electoral Princes are mentioned, it refers to individuals who were empowered to elect the Emperor/Kaiser. The Prince Bishops of Cologne, Mainz and Trier were Bishops who were simultaneously Electors in the Empire; there were other Prince Bishops who were offspring of kings but not Electors.

Where the city of Freiburg is mentioned, it refers to the Swiss city now commonly known by its French name, Fribourg; the German city in the Black Forest, Freiburg im Breisgau is shown with its full name; the German city of *Köln* is given with its English name Cologne. The names Alsace (German: *Elsass*) and Lorraine (German: *Lothringen*) were used in lieu of their old German names because they are more common in modern English. Similarly, the English name for Sigismund was used instead of the German form Siegmund. The city and canton of Lucerne is rendered in both that and its German form, "*Luzern*". German spellings with the "*Umlaut*" over a vowel have been retained but can be easily tracked as: ä = ae, ö = oe and ü = ue; where the German consonant "ß" is retained, it equates to "ss".

---

2 "*Der Löwe von Burgund*".

3 "*Der Engadiner Krieg*".

CHRONOLOGY

12 April 1465: Charles the Bold assumes affairs of state from his father, Philipp the Good

22 May 1467: Nonaggression pact between Burgundy and some Swiss Confederation (German: *Eidgenossenschaft*[4]) cantons

15 June 1467: Philipp the Good dies

28 October 1467: Charles the Bold's victory over the rebellious Liégeois at the Battle of Brustem

October 1468: Renewed uprising of the Liégeois

29-30 October 1468: Nighttime attack of the "600 Franchimontois" on Charles the Bold's Camp

5 September 1469: Treaty of St. Omer: Tyrolean Duke Sigismund (Siegmund) pawns Habsburg lands in the Alsace and other regions to Charles the Bold

20 September 1469: Peter von Hagenbach becomes the Burgundian Steward in the pawned lands

30 March 1474: "Perpetual Accord": Treaty between Duke Sigismund of Tyrol and the Swiss Confederation

11 April 1474: Uprising against Peter von Hagenbach, his arrest

9 May 1474: Hagenbach's execution in Breisach

24 June 1474: Alsatian knights invade the Free County[5] of Burgundy

21 July 1474: Decampment of the Burgundian Army in the Rhineland

30 July 1474: Siege of Neuss begins

18 August 1474: Burgundian forces begin the punitive expedition against Upper Alsace

25 October 1474: Swiss Confederation declares war on Burgundy

13 November 1474: Victory of the Swiss Confederation and its allies over the Burgundian Army under Henri de Neuchâtel-Blamont at Héricourt

9 May 1475: Lorraine's Duke René II declares war on Charles the Bold

11 May 1475: Arrival of the Imperial relief army at Neuss

29 May 1475: Ceasefire between the Burgundians and the Imperial Army

26-27 June 1475: Final withdrawal of the Burgundians at Neuss

19 July 1475: Conquest of l'Isle-Doubs by the Swiss and their allies

9 August 1475: Conquest of Blamont by the Swiss and their allies

13 September 1475: Treaty of Soleuvre between Charles the Bold and the French King Louis XI

14 October 1475: Capture of Murten/Morat by Bernese forces

27 October 1475: "Bad Day of Stäffis": Capture of Estavayer by the Bernese, massacre of the civilian populace

October and November 1475: Complete occupation of Lorraine by the Burgundians

13 November 1475: Battle of La Planta: Victory of Valais and Swiss Confederation over Savoy (allied with Burgundy)

17 November 1475: Marriage agreement regarding Charles' hereditary daughter Maria and Maximilian, the son of Emperor (Kaiser) Frederick III

28 February 1476: Bernese garrison of Grandson capitulates to the Burgundians

29 February 1476: Execution of the Bernese prisoners by Charles the Bold

2 March 1476: Battle of Grandson, defeat of Charles the Bold's Burgundians by the Swiss Confederation and its allies

9 June 1476: Siege of Murten by the Burgundians begins

22 June 1476: Battle of Murten, defeat of Charles the Bold's Burgundians by the Swiss Confederation and its allies

26-27 June 1476: Abduction of Savoy's Duchess on the orders of Charles the Bold; start of the anti-Burgundian uprising in Savoy

6 or 7 October 1476: Burgundian garrison of Nancy surrenders to the Duke of Lorraine

22 October 1476: Arrival of the Burgundian besieging army under Charles the Bold at Nancy

5 January 1477: Battle of Nancy, defeat of Charles the Bold's Burgundians by the Swiss Confederation and its allies; death of Charles the Bold

21 April 1477: Marriage of Maria of Burgundy and Maximilian von Habsburg; large portions of the Burgundian empire go to the house of Habsburg

---

4   The term "Swiss Confederation" used in this book, is the English version of "*Eidgenossenschaft*," literally "oath Association" or "Oath Companionship," and refers to the "Eight Places" or cantons at the time of the Burgundian Wars, i.e., Uri, Schwyz, Unterwalden, Bern, Zug, Zurich (Zürich), Glarus and Lucerne (Luzern). The Allies: Fribourg (Freiburg im Üchtland), Murten, Biel and Solothurn.

5   The term "county" used in this book refers to a territory ruled by a count, i.e., a noble of that rank, rather than in the modern sense of the word. It corresponds to the French term "comté" and the German "*Grafschaft*."

THE DUCHY OF BURGUNDY – THE DUKES OF BURGUNDY

In 1363 the French King John II the Good (French (Fr.): *Jean II le Bon*)[6] of the House of Valois enfeoffed his fourth and youngest son, named Philipp,[7] called "the Bold" (French: Philippe le Hardi) with the Duchy of Burgundy. He took office, as Philipp II, the accession making him the last Duke of Burgundy from the line of the Capetians after Philipp of Rouvres[8]. In 1369 he married Margarete of Flanders, the widow of his predecessor (who died of the plague without being able to consummate the marriage). She brought through various inheritances large properties to the house of Burgundy, which together were decidedly larger than the actual duchy and some of which, like the Free County of Burgundy (*France-Comté*), belonged to the Holy Roman Empire. Thus, Philipp also became a vassal of the Emperor.

Despite his large and in fact largely independent territories he felt above all a member of the French royal family, and after the death of his oldest brother Charles V, called "the Wise" (*Charles VI le Sage*),[9] together with his other brothers initially exercised the governance for his underage nephew Charles VI, called "the Mad" (*Charles VI le Fou*).[10] When the latter became incapable of reigning after a few years, Philipp attempted to regain the levers of power, but found a bitter enemy in his nephew Louis of Orleans (*Louis de Valois, duc d'Orleans*),[11] the King's brother.

The struggles for power in the French court were continued by Philipp's son and heir John the Fearless (Fr.: *Jean sans Peur*),[12] who followed his father in the duke's seat. He completed the unification of his mother's inherited lands with the duchy and began a seesaw policy between France and England that increasingly brought him the status of an independent prince.

John the Fearless' hostility toward Louis of Orleans peaked in 1407 in his murder, and it brought him leadership of French affairs of state as well as responsibility for the upbringing of the Dauphin[13] Louis (*Louis de Valois*).[14] Orleans' affairs with respect to the Dauphin were represented in the meantime by the Armagnac[15] Party. In 1413, it succeeded in taking over power in Paris, upon which John the Fearless sought an alliance with England.

On 10 September 1419 direct negotiations began between the new Dauphin Charles[16] and the Duke of Burgundy whereupon the Dauphin's companions stabbed John to death from behind.

His son Philipp, called "the Good" (*Philippe le Bon*),[17] who as the successor to John the Fearless ascended as Philipp III and in 1420 allied with King Henry V[18] of England who at that time had conquered large parts of France and stood at the height of his power. Philipp's seesaw politics between France and England paid off in the Treaty of Arras when he reconciled with Charles VII. That brought him a series of additional domains within France, but above all it rid him of his vassalage to the French King. With that, Philipp became simultaneously completely independent in the French part of his domains. At the same time and subsequently through inheritances, treaties and military actions, he expanded the territories from the Holy Roman Empire by adding the area of the modern Benelux states, against which Emperor Sigismund protested without success.

With those acquisitions, Philipp the Good ruled an ethnic-linguistic, from a political, legal and geographic perspective, heterogeneous complex of lands on this and the other side of the German-French border.[19] His expanded domain was dynastically based and was reminiscent of the Middle Empire of Emperor Lothar I[20] (albeit without access to the Mediterranean).

---

6 Born 16 April 1319, died 8 April 1364.
7 Born 15 January 1342 in Pontoise, died 27 April 1404 in Halle in the Hennegau/Hainaut, Belgium.
8 Born 1346, died 21 November 1361.
9 Born 21 January 1338, died 16 September 1380.
10 Born March 1368, died 21 October 1422.
11 Born 13 March 1372, died 23 November 1407.
12 Born 28 May 1371 in Dijon, died 10 September 1419 in Montereau-Fault-Yonne.
13 Title of the French heir to the throne at the time of the Valois and Bourbon dynasties.
14 Born 22 January 1397 in Paris, died there 18 December 1415.
15 The Counts of Armagnac were supporters of the House of Orleans. After Louis' murder, his son 13-year old Charles of Orleans was to lead the party. This was taken over by Bernard VII d'Armagnac who recruited an army of mercenaries and who stood out not only because of his exceptional brutality, but also because after that until the 1444 Battle of St. Jakob an der Birs, he struck terror into the people's hearts.
16 The later Charles VII, called "the Victorious" (Charles VII le Victorieux), born 22 February 1403 in Paris, died 22 July 1461 in Mehun-sur-Yévre, was king of France from 1422 to 1461. With the help of the Maid of Orleans (Jeanne d'Arc) he succeeded in turning the Hundred Years War and the final expulsion of the English from France.
17 Born 31 July 1396 in Dijon, died 15 June 1467 in April 1367 in Bruges.
18 Born 16 September 1387 in Monmouth Castle in Wales, died 31 August 1442 at Bois de Vincennes near Paris.
19 This border is, however, not comparable with the national borders in the modern sense. In France, a national centrally governed state began under Charles VII in the following period, and the Holy Roman Empire, which first received the unofficial addition of "of the German Nation" in the second half of the 15th century, was a decidedly multi-ethnic state.
20 Born in 795, died 29 September 855 in the Prüm Abbey, he was king of the Lothari Regnum from 843 to 855 that per the Treaty of Verdun of 10 August 843 formed the middle part of the Carolingian Frankish Empire. This however extended to central Italy. The political-geographic designation "Lorraine" (German "*Lothringen*") is derived from his name.

On 10 January 1430, he created the Order of the Golden Fleece, on the model of the English Order of the Garter, as a unifying device for the elite in his domains and a central point of reference of a courtly culture of its own.

However, his empire actually was divided into two main parts that had no land connection: the northerly, that reached from Picardy northeasterly to Holland and from there southeasterly to Luxembourg, and the southerly, mainly consisting of the actual Duchy of Burgundy, the Free county and the county of Nevers. In between lay the French Champagne and the Lorraine belonging to the Empire.

And starting in 1475, Philipp's son, Charles I, the Bold (*Charles I le Téméraire* or *Charles I le Hardi*)[21] tried to incorporate the latter lands into his empire.

Duke Charles the Bold (old Dutch engraving)

On 12 April 1465, i.e., a good two years before Philipp III's death, Charles had already taken over the affairs of state from his father. He continued not only his ostentatious court and knightly culture[22], but also his policies of expansion. In military activities, he showed himself to be a personally brave but also brutal war captain who did not shy away from committing a bloodbath among populaces he conquered. Representative of this were his actions against Liège that rebelled repeatedly against Burgundian rule – with dramatic consequences. The Prince-Bishopric of Liège was at a strategic location. Therefore, occupying the Bishop's seat was a political matter of European dimension. In 1456, under Burgundian pressure, the 18-year old Louis of Bourbon[23] became the Prince-Bishop of Liège. On 22 November 1455 under Burgundian pressure, the Liège Cathedral Chapter had deposed the old Bishop, John VIII of Heinsberg. Now Louis de Bourbon, with the support of the Duke of Burgundy and the Pope –then Callixtus III – became the new Bishop. During his time in office there were repeatedly conflicts with the burghers of Liège. Again, the rich city was in danger of losing its former independence, because it was essentially surrounded by Burgundian territory. With the support of the King of France, Louis XI, the Liégeois drove out their Bishop who fled to Maastricht. The Liégeoises chose Markus von Baden,[24] son of the Margrave Jakob I von Baden as their new Bishop.[25] However, the military support they promised was marginal in the face of Burgundy's strength. Charles the Bold, still an heir to the throne, was already busy elsewhere with military operations, so Duke Philipp, despite his advanced age, gathered the Burgundian force himself and defeated the numerically superior forces of Liège under Raes van Heers[26] at the Battle of Montenaken (Belgium) on 20 October 1465. That finally led to the Peace of Saint-Trond on 22 December 1465. Louis de Bourbon returned to power, the Prince-Bishopric was forced to pay more than 300,000 guilders to Burgundy as reparations,[27] and it became a Burgundian protectorate. In August 1466 Charles the Bold conquered the Walloon city of Dinant and held a gruesome, punitive trial of its inhabitants– hundreds of the city's burghers were drowned in the Maas (Meuse) River.[28]

---

22 The financial foundations for these were, among others, the taxes from Flemish cities that had gotten rich from the textile industry.

23 He was the nephew of Duke Phillip and thus Charles the Bold's cousin. He was born in 1438; he died on 30 August 1482 in Liège.

24 Born in 1434; died on 1 September 1478.

25 See Seldner, Heinrich, *Lüttich, die zweite burgundische Dynastie und die Markgrafen Karl und Markus von Baden, 1455-1468* (Rastatt, 1865), p. 34.

26 Actually Raes van der Rivieren, Baron of Heers and Linter. He was born around 1418 and died on 25 October 1477.

27 The City of Liège had to raise the money.

28 See Blockmanns, William and Prevenier, Walter, *The Promised Lands: The Low Countries Under Burgundian Rule, 1369-1530* (Philadelphia: University of Pennsylvania Press, 1999), p. 180.

---

21 Born 10 November 1433 in Dijon, died 5 January 1477 at Nancy.

Burgundy under Philipp the Good Map: Marco Zanoli and Bernhard Glänzer

Indeed, after the death of Philipp the Good in June 1467, the Liège citizenry – encouraged by French emissaries - threw the gauntlet at the Bishop and his Burgundian allies. Charles the Bold, in the meantime having become the Duke of Burgundy, reengaged by his cousin Louis, gathered an army of about 25,000 men and attacked Liège's army – about 12,000 infantry and 500 horsemen under Raes van Heers – at the Battle of Brusthem on 28 October 1467. Burgundian and Liégeois artillery played an important role there.[29] Charles the Bold concentrated his bowmen and dismounted knights in the center and mounted forces on the wings, also as his reserve. The first attack made on foot, supported by artillery, immediately penetrated the Liégeois fortifications at Brusthem. But a counterattack by Liege's pikemen threw back the Burgundians who lost 400 to 500 men dead. Then Charles employed the bowmen from his reserve, and Liège's battle formation collapsed and its forces fled. Only the advent of dusk prevented further losses from being far greater.[30] The Liégeois left 3,000 to 4,000 dead on the battlefield. On 12 November, Liege surrendered and received a Burgundian governor, Guy de Humbercourt. But the Burgundian rule was still not secure. In October 1468, 240 rebels under the leadership of Jean de Wilde, Vincent de Bueren and Gosuin de Streel, forced their way into the city. Humbercourt and his Burgundian soldiers fled, and Jean de Wilde moved into the Prince-Bishop's palace. The Liégeois took Tongeren in a night attack and killed all the Burgundians there. Then Jean de Wilde entered negotiations with Guy de Humbercourt. But in the meantime Charles the Bold had decided to end the Liégeois resistance for good. French King Louis XI just happened to be visiting Charles' army. The King had gone to Charles the Bold' cantonment in Péronne for negotiations, and just then they received news of the Liégeois uprising (that the French King had goaded into rebelling through two emissaries). King Louis was now the Duke of Burgundy's de facto prisoner, who forced the Treaty of Péronne upon him and made him accompany him on the punitive expedition against Liège. On the way, Burgundian soldiers stormed Tongeren. On 22 October, 500 Liégeois militiamen attempted to delay the Burgundian army at the town of Lantin. They were driven into the church and burned alive. Vincent de Bueren organized Liège's defense and achieved some minor successes with some sorties. Jean de Wilde was fatally wounded during such a sortie on 26 October and died two days later. The nighttime attack of the "600 Franchimontois"[31] on the night of 29-30 October is well known. The Liégeois troops were initially able to leave the city unnoticed and attacked the Burgundians. Their objective was to overrun the quarters of the Duke and the French King – who must have seemed a traitor to them - and kill both of them. The plan failed. All of them, including, Vincent de Bueren and Gosuin de Streel, were killed.[32] The next day Liege surrendered, Duke Charles had the city plundered and laid waste. Hundreds of Liégeois were bound together and thrown into the Maas/Meuse River. Supposedly the city burned for seven days. But the resistance in Wallonia was still not completely extinguished. Charles the Bold developed an unforgiving hatred of the Imperial cities that he tended to underestimate. Similarly, from then on at the latest, the French King strove to destroy Charles. But Charles considered himself superior to his opponents.

From the start of his rule, Charles was very busy with reorganizing his administration and the military. In addition to the defense establishment resting on the medieval feudal system, over time he maintained larger mercenary units, especially from England and Italy. He is said to have created military-technical, organizational and disciplinary concepts almost daily. With the "Ordonnance"[33] of 19 April 1472, he designated nobles from his court as leaders of his "Ordonnance" companies and militarized the court in the subsequent period by further meshing the court with the army. His main enemy was – at least after Liege's devastation – the French King Louis XI,[34] against whom he went to battle[35] on 16 July 1465. Both parties sought allies in the following years. Charles allied himself with Edward V of England,[36] whose sister Margaret of York, he married on 3 July 1468. King Louis in turn especially drew the Swiss to his side who fought a series of successful battles against Charles the Bold. In the north, Charles' efforts to realign the borders of his territories by incorporating the Duchy of Guelders[37] into his group of

---

29 See DeVries, Kelly and Smith, Robert Douglas, *Medieval Military Technology* (Toronto: University of Toronto Press, 2012), p. 145.

30 See Heath, Ian, *Armies of the Middle Ages, Volume 1* (Worthing: Wargames Research Group, 1982), p. 82.

31 See Gaier, Claude, *Art et organization militaires dans la principauté de Liège et dans le comté de Looz au Moyen âge* (Brussels: Académie Royale de Belgique, 1968), p. 154.

32 The "600 Franchimontois" and their heroic act of arms belong to the Belgian national mythos. Whether the small Franchimont barony could raise 600 armed men is very doubtful.

33 The French term *"ordonnace"*, i.e., ordinance or regulation, referred to a set of rules establishing the deployment and the collaboration of various fighting forces at the end of the Middle Ages. In French they were referred to as *"Ordonnance"* and in German *"Ordonnanz"*. Thus, the *ordonnance* companies should be thought of as military structures that were organized in accordance with a set of rules – a departure from how the medieval armies were constituted.

34 Louis XI, *le prudent* (the Careful), also called *"l'araignée"* (the Spider); born 3 July 1423 in Bourges, died 30 August 1483 at Plessis-lès-Tours, King of France from 1461 to 1483. He was named this for his intrigues. In German history books he is sometimes called *"Ludwig XI. Der Kluge"* (Louis XI the Clever).

35 The Battle of Montlhéry ended in a draw, however it led to Louis having to make significant concessions.

36 Born 28 April 1442 in Rouen; died 9 April 1483; was King of England from 1461 to 1470 and from 1471 to 1483.

37 Guelders or Gueldres (Dutch: *Gelre*, German: *Geldern*) is a historical county, later a duchy of the Holy Roman Empire, located in the Low Countries.

Franchimont Castle
Photo: Marko Tjemmes

states were initially crowned with success. What was not successful was his attempt to become a king. Because Charles the Bold had no male heirs, he demanded that his daughter Marie de Bourgogne[38] (Maria of Burgundy) be married to the Emperor's son Archduke Maximilian,[39] as had been agreed to with Emperor Frederick III[40] in Trier on 30 September 1473. A coronation to the Roman-German King was out of the question because it would have made him the Emperors successor. Why the possibility of coronation with the crown of a newly created Kingdom of Burgundy or Friesland failed has not been clearly explained. In any case Charles once intended to expand further into the Holy Roman Empire in that he intervened in the Bishops' feud in Cologne (Köln) and besieged Neuss for ten months starting in July 1474.

---

38 Born 13 February 1457 in Brussels, died 27 March 1482 in Bruges, daughter of Charles the Bold from his second marriage with his cousin, Isabelle de Bourbon (born 1437, died 25 September 1465 in Antwerp).

39 Born 22 March 1459 in Wiener Neustadt, died 12 January 1519 in Wels, Upper Austria; starting 1477 was Duke of Burgundy, starting 1486 was Roman-German King, and starting 1508 the Emperor of the Holy Roman empire.

40 Born 21 September 1415 in Innsbruck; died 19 August 1493 in Linz; from the House of Habsburg. Starting in 1440 he was the Roman-German King and starting in 1452 the Emperor of the Holy Roman Empire.

THE SIEGE OF NEUSS

In 1474 Charles the Bold had an (allegedly) good opportunity to expand his sphere of power eastward and thus finally to rise to the circle of European great powers.

On 30 March 1463, Ruprecht von der Pfalz, the younger brother of the powerful Electoral Prince Friedrich I von der Pfalz, was chosen to be the Archbishop of Cologne. His predecessor, Dietrich von Moers, had so heavily indebted the *Erzstift*,[41] i.e., the Bishop's secular domain, that after his death a large part of this area's estates decided to form a *Erblandesvereinigung* (Union of Hereditary Lands) and to not recognize any nobles who, before he took office, had not agreed to guarantee the estates' rights. This included, among other things, all the important financial, political and military decisions that the Electoral Prince could make only with the concurrence of the estates. Among the latter was the Cologne Cathedral's Chapter (*Kölner Domkapitel*), which as a committee could force each candidate for the election to be the archbishop' seat to recognize this agreement. Thus, Ruprecht attested to the *Erblandesvereinigung* but after only a few years he did not comply with it but got involved with military conflicts with the incumbents of some of his predecessors' mortgaged properties. In the conflict about the levying of a head-and-hearth tax, he took the Zons *Zollfestung (Zons Customs/Tax Fortress)* and tried to capture the city of Neuss. The Estates deposed him in short order and in the spring of 1473 chose Hermann von Hessen, a member of the Cathedral's Chapter, to be the "Captain and Protector of the Bishopric" ("*Hauptmann und Beschirmer der Erzstiftes*"), in other words the Bishopric's administrator.

However, Ruprecht was unwilling to accept that. He still had a certain amount of backing from a few smaller landed Estates and at least had one powerful ally outside his own former territories, namely his brother Frederick the Count of the Palatine (*Pfalzgraf*) on the Rhine and Electoral Prince of the Palatine (*Kurfürst von der Pfalz*). But even his support was not enough, so Ruprecht went to the neighboring Duchy of Guelders and requested assistance from the landed lords there who had recently mortgaged properties there.[42] This dealt with far smaller, less important landowners than Duke Charles I.[43] And he did not wait particularly long to ask the very disempowered Archbishop and Electoral Prince to name him the administrative steward of the Bishopric (*Erzstift*) and he took over the "defense of his rights".[44] Thus Charles the Bold already possessed the official title of the Elector of Cologne before he was able to actually realize his expansionist aims.

To do this he initially used various methods: in Cologne he had a herald make a public proclamation that the Cathedral Chapter and the other Landed Estates had to instantly submit to Electoral Prince Ruprecht, while the city of Neuss was looking to get negotiators for its side. His emissary delegation, under Lord Robert of Arburg, whom the Neuss residents would not let leave the city, were dealt with between an outer and inner city gate. In the event Neuss was willing to be under the protection of the Duke, the delegation even supposedly promised future "imperial immediacy"[45] status. Neuss rejected the offer with the note that they had sent the entire matter to the Emperor and the Pope and had to wait for their decision. The Cologne citizens tore down the notices as well as the ducal coats of arms and tread them into the mud.

With that, the signs of war were clear. The Burgundian forces gathered in Maastricht from where they departed toward the Rhine on 21 July 1474. The Cologners, who had had already sent pleas for assistance to the Emperor and to Count Heinrich of Hessen, the Bishopric Administrator's brother, wrote "The Duke of Burgundy departed today with his army, wanting, as one says, to take Neuss or Cologne."[46] Because Cologne - with its surface area of 400 hectares, its kilometer long Rhine bank and its strong artillery - was also nearly impossible to surround even with Charles' powerful forces, he chose to turn to Neuss.[47] Neuss' calls for help to the Emperor and Protector of the Bishopric resulted in the latter arriving on 26 July with

---

41 In German-speaking parts of medieval Europe, an *Erzstift* referred to the territory ruled by a prince-archbishop.

42 Löhrer, Friedrich J., *Geschichte der Stadt Neuss von Ihrer Gründung an bis jetzt* (Neuss: Druck und Verlag E. Schwann, 1840).

43 Duke Charles had intervened in a civil war between the Duke of Guelders, Arnold of Egmont, and his son Adolf as a supporter for Arnold. Because Arnold could not succeed in establishing his claims in those areas in Guelders that belonged to his son, he mortgaged the duchy to Charles the Bold for 300,000 guilders in 1471. Charles then forced his control over Guelders militarily until 1473.

44 "*Vertheidigung seines Rechtes*", i.e., to essentially have control of the laws. See Löhrer, p. 141.

45 Ibid, p. 143. Imperial immediacy (German: *Reichsfreiheit* or *Reichsunmittelbarkeit*) was a privileged constitutional and political status rooted in German feudal law under which the Imperial estates of the Holy Roman Empire such as Imperial cities, prince-bishoprics and secular principalities, and individuals such as the Imperial knights, were declared free from the authority of any local lord and placed under the direct ("immediate", in the sense of "without an intermediary") authority of the Emperor, and later of the institutions of the Empire such as the Diet (*Reichstag*), the Imperial Chamber of Justice and the Aulic Council. Source: Wikipedia.

46 In Middle High German (MHG) "*Der Hertzog von Burgundien ist hude zu Tricht uffgebrochen mit syme heer, in willen, als man sagt, Nuysse oder Colne zu belegen.*" Ulrich, Adolf, "*Akten zum Neusser Kriege 1472-1475*" in *Annalen der historischen Vereins für den Niederrhein*, 49 (Hannover: Hofdruckerei der Gebrüder Jänecke, 1889), p. 13.

47 See Metsdorf, Jens, "*Bedrängnis, Angst und große Mühsal*" – *Die Belagerung von Neuss durch Karl den Kühnen 1474/75*, in: "... würfen hin in steine/gröze und niht kleine... Belagerungen und Belagerungsanlagen im Mittelalter" (*Beihefte zur Mediaevistik, Bd. 7*) (Frankfurt a. M.: Olaf Wagener, 2006), pp. 167-188.

70 knights, 300 horsemen and 1,500 foot solders. That was three days before the scouting force of the besieging estimated 15,000[48] man strong Burgundian Army was first sighted.

Siege of Neuss
From the Chronicle of Conradius von Pfettisheim

Although Neuss was only a fraction of the size of Cologne, it had exceptional defensive capabilities due to its topographic location and its both extensive and modern fortifications. Located on hills for the most part, since the 12th century it had a city wall surrounded by a moat. Since the middle of the 15th century these defenses had been supplemented with a whole system of defensive works built with the most recent concepts of the science of fortifications. Its key feature was having two water-filled moats with an earth barrier between them. The two moats were fed by local sources, primarily from the Erft and Knur Rivers. Additionally, there were further redoubts and palisades, many towers along the walls and five city gates that were like small fortresses. The defensive belt was 50 meters (164 feet) wide in some places.[49] When word arrived about the approach of the Burgundian army and during the first days of the siege, the defenses were further strengthened. Food and munitions for many days were on hand so that the city's inhabitants and defenders could confidently resist. The latter consisted of an estimated 5,000 men under arms[50] at the beginning of the siege along with the city's able-bodied burghers and the Bishopric Administrator's Hessian soldiers, plus the levies from the cities of Cologne and Bonn and various mercenary units.

On 30 July, Charles the Bold's forces initially began to construct the ring of siege works, whereby the core of his troops – 3,000 Burgundian horsemen and 1,000 Burgundian foot soldiers – started in front of the powerful *Obertor* (Watergate) on the city's southern end. Contingents from other parts of his empire – Liégeois, Flemish and Dutch among others - arrived further to the north. Several thousand troops from Lombardy and other Italian mercenaries closed up the semi-circle in the north, while 2,000 Englishmen occupied the *Hammfeld* arc southeast of the *Obertor*.

The Duke set up his headquarters in front of that gate in the garden of the *Oberkloster* (Upper Monastery) that the Neuss residents had not fully destroyed before his arrival. In no way did he give up holding court and displays of splendor that seemed appropriate to him. He resided in a tent-like structure with wood paneling and fireplaces in which he not only led the war effort but also affairs of state. He received diplomats and crowned leaders, conducted learned conversations and readings from books here – all under the protection of his 500-man strong bodyguard who were recruited from the core of his Burgundian troops. A city of market stalls to pander to the army's civilian retinue sprung up in the area around this camp that was protected by palisades and ditches. These market stalls supposedly had more buildings than all of Neuss. Almost anything in the way of goods and services that the soldiers and mercenaries might want was offered here.

In mid-August 1474 Lombard and Picardy forces were able to seize the "Werth" and "Waid" islands that both lay between Erft Canal and the Rhine that flowed directly by the city. This completed the siege ring around the city and cut off the last supply route to Neuss. However, it did not give the besiegers one hundred percent control of the waters bordering the city. Even after that, time and again messengers were able sneak through the lines at night in both directions.

Charles the Bold's attempts to drain the city's moats remained unsuccessful. Although the hundreds of ditch-diggers, including women, employed to redirect the flow of the Erft and Knur Rivers were successful in doing so, the numerous springs in and around Neuss were sufficient to maintain the water level in the moats.[51]

---

48 The numbers vary between 13,000 and 30,000 men depending on the sources. See information about the numbers in Lange, Joseph, *Pulchra Nussia. "Die Belagerung der Stadt Neuss durch Herzog Karl den Kühnen von Burgund 1474/75"*, in *Neuss, Burgund und das Reich (Schriftenreihe des Stadtarchivs Neuss, Bd. 6)* (Neuss: Stadtarchiv, 1975), p. 28f.

49 See Bömmels, Nicolaus, *"Die Neusser unter dem Druck der Belagerung"*, in *Neuss, Burgund und das Reich (Schriftenreihe des Stadtarchivs Neuss, Bd. 6)* (Neuss: Stadtarchiv, 1975).

50 See Lange, Joseph, *Pulchra Nussia*, p. 40.

51 Ibid., p. 43.

So, in mid-August, the Burgundians began to systematically bombard the city with artillery of all calibers up to 40 cm (16 inches). The portions of the defensive works destroyed at this time could be replaced with field fortifications as needed but the barrages resulted in many casualties and began to demoralize the defenders.

It fell to Hermann von Hessen, as the Bishopric Administrator and City Commandant, in addition to his military tasks in the narrow sense, to repeatedly motivate the people and to ensure the security of those shut in the city. He was aided by his closeness to the people and by his having declared martial law at the beginning of the siege, which was visible to everyone in the form of a gallows and a breaking wheel.[52]

After more than three weeks of artillery barrages, Charles the Bold had his army begin to assault Neuss on 10 September. For a total of seven hours his troops attacked the Rhine Gate (*Rheintor*) and Water Gate (*Obertor*) with enormous losses. Then summoning up all their strength, the defenders - including women and children who brought materials for the defense like hot water and boiling pitch to the front-most lines – were able to fend off the attack.

At this time the defenders had no idea that some of them who would survive the siege would experience a total of 56 of such assaults.

In doing so, they did not limit themselves to just defensive measures, but used every opportunity to cost the enemy losses and damage through sorties. As early as 29 September they initiated a surprise attack on the Burgundian encampment. They started from two gates and captured cannon, hand-cannon, as well as tons of gunpowder and in the end also set fire to the Burgundian tents. The chronicler Christian Wierstraet wrote that the soldiers "fresh and happily sprung back into the city".[53] In this way they were able to temporarily get some breathing room.

But the Burgundians' repertoire was not limited to assaults and artillery barrages. They breathed down the city's neck with "newly created means",[54] for example gunpowder-filled wooden pipes, i.e., explosives, flaming arrows, that started a city fire in October. They exploited the resulting chaos to attempt a renewed assault, but the ensuing wind-blown cinders ignited a major fire in the Lombard tent camp that not only destroyed many weapons and tools but also cost the lives of many people and horses.

To prevent sudden attacks by the Neuss forces, Charles' people dug deep ditches in front of the city gates and piled up the soil as walls. At the same time they began to dig mines under the city's defenses.

Attacks and counterattacks followed one another. However, the Burgundians could replace their significantly higher losses[55] with fresh troops. So, at the beginning of November they immediately began an attack on the Rhine Gate with new contingents from Flanders and Brabant with a "turtle" ("*Katze*").[56]

After three months of besieging, while Charles the Bold had made no significant progress toward his goal despite enormous numeric superiority and almost unlimited supplies of men and material, the besieged city noticed its first signs of shortages. The shortage of wood to burn that began in October was initially dealt with by limiting themselves to two kitchens and by only using wood from old houses. However, in the first half of November, gunpowder was becoming scarce, a shortage that could not be rectified without external assistance. On 10 November, the Neuss burghers Johann Hellenbroich and Hinrich van Loe were able to surreptitiously leave the city and take a plea for gunpowder to Cologne. The Cologners provided not only the needed quantities of saltpeter, but also 550 soldiers. The soldiers departed Cologne on 18 November. In addition to their personal equipment, each of them carried a ten-pound sack of the material indispensible for producing the black powder. To get to Neuss, they marched in a northwesterly arc and waited for a night in the village of Liedberg before they headed for Neuss. There are many versions of how they got through the Burgundian lines. Knowledge of the password, disguises as newly arrived Burgundian troops (after all they arrived from the west) or also a certain carelessness in the Duke's army due to many rumors of peace negotiations were provided as reasons. In any case they arrived safely in Neuss on 19 November which significantly strengthened the defenders' resilience not just materially but also psychologically. The psychological effect was also heightened in that the added supplies arrived on St. Elizabeth's Day, because the City Commandant, Hermann von Hessen, was her direct descendant.

For the inhabitants of Liedberg, who had provided lodging to the Cologne troops on their way to Neuss, the episode ended in a catastrophe. Charles the Bold torched and razed the village and 300 inhabitants died.

---

52 The breaking wheel or execution wheel, also known as the Catherine wheel or simply the Wheel, was a torture method used for public execution from antiquity through Middle Ages into the early modern period by breaking a criminal›s bones and/or bludgeoning them to death. Source: Wikipedia.

53 In MHG "*vrysch ind vroelych weder in dye stat sprongen*".

54 In MHG "*nuwen erdachten manyeren*".

55 A Nuremberg chronicler speaks of 7,000 men in this context.

56 A "*Katze*" (cat), called a "turtle" or "tortoise" in English was a movable protective shelter of wood or wicker in which troops could approach a fortification under protection. By the Middle Ages it was actually already old technology. It was a protected siege engine designed to break or circumvent heavy castle doors, thick city walls and other fortifications, and it essentially consisted of a battering ram inside a mobile shed.

Firing a light cannon
Photo: Susan Sümer

At the end of December food began to become scarce in Neuss. Compulsory controls included all meat supplies and forced the burghers to deliver them to supply the military. At the end, only three cows remained "so that one had milk [only] for the small children"[57] and for the sick according to Wiersraet, the city scribe.

While slowly but surely hunger increased in Neuss, there was no shortage of provisions in the Burgundian army. Despite the Emperor expressly forbidding it, the Duke of Jülich-Berg regularly supplied the Burgundians and thus contributed to their ability to continue the siege.

But Charles' means were not inexhaustible. Despite various special taxes that he imposed in his lands, he was temporarily unable to pay the weekly salaries for his troops and mercenaries. He supposedly then ordered assaults on the city in which the unpaid troops had to fight in the front ranks and were thus decimated.

When on 6 January 1475 a section of the outer city wall by the Rhine Gate crashed into the moat with a loud roar, the Burgundians' way into the city seemed open. But the Neuss defenders were able to seal it in a makeshift manner with a temporary bulwark – using wine casks, gabions and other materials.

Since November Duke Charles had already been having construction materials continuously brought from Maastricht and Liège. The counter-bulwarks and attack towers built by his personnel soon towered over Neuss' defenses and contributed significantly to the defenders' losses of their bastions. It is known that Charles employed the technical know-how of at least four trained miners in constructing tunnels. But Neuss also had a specialist in its ranks, a miner from Liège, who performed invaluable service by detecting the tunnels. Among the modern warfare techniques the Burgundians employed was using favorable winds to produce smoke screens to screen their attacks.

On 20 January, a flood forced the Burgundians to evacuate Werth Island. Neuss was able to recover the material left behind, including cannon, handguns, gunpowder and foodstuffs. What they could not carry off, they burned or sank in the Rhine. At the same time they prepared for the expected street and house-to-house fighting by dig-

---

57   In MHG, *"daevon men hade milch vur die cleine kynderchen"*.

ging floodable ditches and creating passageways between houses. On 7 February they held a jousting tournament in the marketplace in order to deceive the enemy about the terrible conditions; Wierstraet described a first part as slaughtering of horses.[58] In all 350 were killed eventually in order to save the lives of the trapped humans.

After the bastions protecting the Rhine Gate and Water Gate were lost with heavy casualties on both sides, the Neuss garrison sent an appeal for help to Cologne on 12 February. The letter not only described their questionable situation,[59] but for the first time gave a deadline of eight days in which they needed to be relieved in order to avoid being forced into surrender negotiations with the Burgundian Duke.

The appeal did not miss its goal. On 18 February, 2,000 Cologne troops arrived on the "Stones" ("*Steine*") on the right side of the Rhine across from Neuss. That alone evoked celebrating in the besieged city. The Cologners, whose contingent grew to 4,000 men over the next days, was joined by a – primarily symbolic – force of Imperial soldiers. They shot up and seized Burgundian ships and joined the fighting with artillery barrages on the other side of the Rhine. This was indeed noteworthy support for the defenders who again dared to make a sortie onto Werth Island, but Cologne's action was not a genuine relief. The troops did not cross the river to engage in the fighting as infantry. Furthermore, most of these "soldiers" were conscripted burghers without any prior wartime experience and were of little fighting value. The solders from Cologne and also the mercenaries deserted in droves[60] after they were attacked by Charles the Bold's forces. In the end there were not even 700 men who could maintain contact with Neuss' forces.

The Burgundian attacks were intensified further after the arrival of the forces from Cologne. During the last weeks of February the Duke personally led his multiethnic army in the fighting and attacked the city from all directions. The hardships and high losses also left their marks on his troops. The soldiers were depressed, and the Duke was so angry that he chased the traders out of the encampment but also forced them to leave their money to pay for new troops. In the war council there was talk of halting the siege and withdrawing, which the Duke forbade.

In response to further requests for assistance from Neuss on 18 March 1475, Electoral Prince Albrecht von Brandenburg began a ship-borne diversionary attack from Cologne against Werth Island[61] with 3,000 men. It was to distract the Burgundians from transport ships loaded with food, munitions and equipment destined for the city. But the latter were too slow or loaded too late so that the entire undertaking had to be called off.

In the following period the Burgundians were able to dry out a portion of the city moat or fill it with dirt so they could bring their siege towers closer to the city wall. The most important part of the offensive strategy was a large tunnel that had been moving forward for weeks and whose progress Duke Charles had monitored personally and at risk to his own life, according to Court Chronicler Jean Molinet.

This deadly threat had not gone unnoticed by the Neuss defenders. They build a "counter-mine" that eventually was only separated from the enemy tunnel by a thin layer of earth. On 10 April a group of volunteers broke through this layer of earth and were able to capture the tunnel, named "*lumbartzloch*" (MHG for Lombard Hole) after its Lombard builders, and to drive the Burgundians from it.

On 9 April Neuss had reached an internal crisis. After nine months of siege, increasingly fierce fighting, catastrophic supply shortages and a desperate general situation, the defenders' nerves were raw. A "major discord" (MHG: "*groysse zweydracht*") broke out in the market place. Six hundred armed men cursed at and threatened one another. Who was opposing whom and the exact reason for this turmoil was not recorded. The city commandant, Hermann von Hessen, who wanted to calm the feelings, was himself loudly verbally attacked. He put an end to the critical situation by having the alarm bell in the Quirinius Cathedral rung, whereupon the quarrelers returned to their defenders' posts. This was not the only mob ("*upleuf*") in the city, but the Bishopric Administrator succeeded again and again in defusing the situations.

In the meantime, the not especially combat-effective Cologne troops on the "Stones" on the Rhine were reinforced by units of the Imperial Army that were initially slowly arriving in small numbers. Their core eventually was composed of 2,000 well-armed and motivated horsemen provided by Duke Albrecht of Saxony as well as from the Imperial Cities of Augsburg and Strassburg (French: Strasbourg).

But there were many rivalries and a series of desertions within the reinforcements sent by the Emperor. The reinforcements were of little value to those besieged in Neuss.

While the fighting continued to rage in and around the badly damaged defense works and the Neuss defenders, lacking munitions, had to use paving stones from the streets as projectiles, the allied troops on the Rhine's east bank used a completely new means of communicating with the city. On 21 April, the desperate Neuss defend-

---

58 In Old Frankish, "*perd yrs levens qwijt*", roughly "horses lost their lives".

59 The list ranged from describing collecting mussels and herbs in the city moats to obtain foodstuffs, to the military and defense equipment they lacked, to feared mutiny among the auxiliary troops.

60 Just in the night of 10 to 11 March, 400 conscripts from the artisans' guilds disappeared.

61 There are many versions of the exact objective of the attack, its events and the numbers of troops.

ers held another Rogation[62] procession to the Chapel of the Mater Dolorosa near the *Obertor*. The troops on the east bank fired a hollow cannonball into the hermetically sealed city. A letter inside the cannonball informed Neuss that the Emperor, various Electoral Princes, princes and Imperial cities had gathered "with great, notable folk on horse and foot and so forth"[63] and with weapons and equipment. Additional princes and cities were marching there including the Landed Count Heinrich von Hessen, the brother of the city commandant, with 8,000 men. They all intended to relieve the city in the coming weeks.

This news certainly gave the besieged new hope, but it did not provide practical help. On 8 May, the Neuss defenders replied by the same means, but had to scrape spilt gunpowder off the walls to load the cannon. Hermann von Hessen's situation report showed great desperation, describing the heavy fighting between the *Obertor* and the Customs Gate (*Zolltor*), the extreme shortages of able-bodied men, drinking water, weapons, munitions, foodstuffs and materiel. The most significant problem was, however, the discord that had developed among the defenders. Hermann von Hessen was about to give up because of it.

Three days later, on 11 May 1475, the shut-ins sighted the Imperial Army at Zons. Starting on the 15th of May they noticed that Charles' forces were clearly avoiding the Imperial forces. On 20 May the Imperial Army began to advance from Zons toward Neuss, on 23 May it reached Grimlinghausen and the Erft River where it halted for the first time and formed a wagon laager. Charles had been waiting for that. He advanced over the Erft and took the laager under artillery fire but was finally pushed back to the left side of the Erft. In the following days there were smaller skirmishes and construction of defenses on both sides of the Erft while the papal legate Alexander Numai, Bishop of Forli, worked out a ceasefire. It went into effect on 28 May. A peace treaty followed on 29 May in which the Duke of Burgundy agreed to begin withdrawing his forces on 31 May. In Neuss, where they had been informed about the treaty on 30 May, the populace celebrated the end of the siege with a thanksgiving service. In the following days many members of the three parties made peaceful visits to the opponents' camp or city, whether out of shear curiosity or to spy on the other side.

But Charles the Bold, who stood undefeated before Neuss, was for the present time not thinking of withdrawing his troops. He initially demanded a guarantee that the Imperial Army would not invade his lands and thus forced further negotiations while at the same time he cut off the city from the outside world. On June 5 he obtained better conditions including a one-year ceasefire to protect his lands.

In Neuss they took a breath when the Legate announced the concluding of the treaty. The burghers were "taken into the Emperor's and the Pope's hands" and they paid honor to their representatives who took up residence in the city. The city's defenders, insofar as they were not Neuss burghers, mostly departed. Among them was also the former city commandant, Hermann von Hessen. On June 8, the Neuss populace began destroying the enemy fortifications surrounding the city. From 9 to 13 June the Burgundian forces left their old camp, however, not without setting it ablaze as a farewell. In any case, they only withdrew as far as the Erft where they halted for a longer time in view of the Imperial forces. On 11 June Duke Charles met with Electoral Prince Albrecht of Brandenburg and submitted to him that he would only finally withdraw when the Emperor withdrew. Frederick III then forbade any further interaction with the Burgundians, especially the sale of food to them. The Burgundians then once again pressed forward to the Werth Island in order to secure their transport ships that were lying there, which aroused Neuss and the Cologners who were still on the Rhine's right bank. They pushed back the Burgundians and captured almost a dozen ships on which they found not only important war materials but also a real treasure in valuables like silverware and silks belonging to Duke Charles. The cargo was assessed as being worth over 100,000 guilders. But on Emperor Frederick's orders, the two cities had to hand over the ships and all the cargo because the Burgundians had promised the Emperor they would withdraw his army four miles further in exchange for return of his property. For the Cologners "almost nothing"[64] of the booty remained, and on 26 June the ships departed in the direction of Nijmegen and on the 27th, Charles the Bold set his army in motion toward his homeland. On 28 June the Imperial Army also departed in the direction of Cologne.

---

62 Rogation days are days of prayer and fasting in Western Christianity. They are observed with processions and the Litany of the Saints. The minor rogations are held on Monday to Wednesday preceding Ascension Thursday; the so-called major rogation is held on 25 April. Source: https://en.wikipedia.org/wiki/Rogation_days.

63 In MHG *"mit groissem myrcklicken volke zu perde ind zo voisse..."*.

64 MHG: "vast kleven".

UNREST IN ALSACE AND THE HIGH RHINE[65]

The actual "Burgundian Wars" naturally do not by any means include all the military conflicts in which Duke Charles the Bold was involved. Actually, in the narrower sense the Burgundian Wars were more about the Duke's war against the Swiss Confederation and its allies. That conflict can above all be traced back to the sophisticated and unscrupulous policies of the French King Louis XI who used money, promises and diplomacy to defeat his arch enemy, in contrast to the Empire's ruler who only carried on the Imperial war against the Burgundian Duke with half measures.

Completely in contrast to the centuries-old enmity between the Swiss Confederation and the House of Habsburg, the relationship between the Duchy of Burgundy and the Swiss Confederation had not been hostile for an extended time. Swiss mercenaries – in small numbers – also fought in the Burgundian Army. As late as 1466, Charles the Bold had sought an alliance with the Confederation. This did not come about. But on 22 May 1467 the Burgundian Duke concluded a friendship and non-aggression pact with the cities of Zurich, Bern, Freiburg im Uechtland[66] (Fr.: Fribourg) and Solothurn. Yet the Burgundian Duke often made territorial claims and the Duke was far too ready to carry them out with force, but these claims were not against the Swiss Confederation.

In 1468 the free Imperial city of Mülhausen[67] in Alsace declared war against Duke Sigismund of Tyrol after it had already been in conflict for a long time with nobles of the surrounding Upper Alsace (in the so-called *Sechsplappertkrieg* of 1465-66).[68] As the Duke of Tyrol, Sigismund was the regent of the Austrian outlands that included the Upper Alsace among other territories. Two years earlier, Bern and Solothurn had concluded a defensive and offensive treaty with Mülhausen and so they joined in the fight. Therefore, the Bernese under Niklaus Zurkinden advanced with newly arrived forces into the Habsburg's Sundgau[69] and then on into the Vosges Mountains and destroyed 16 castles and 160 villages. Forces from Solothurn occupied the exceptionally strong Landskron Castle in Sundgau, but they did not succeed in capturing Thann.[70] Schaffhausen, whose environs had been badly devastated by the fighting, turned to the entire Swiss Confederation for help, against which Duke Sigismund declared hostilities. Fifteen thousand Swiss assembled on the Ochsenfeld under the leadership of Adrian von Bubenberg and in the face of this powerful force, the nobles did not risk a battle.

But 300 of the Habsburg's horsemen attacked a supply column from Mülhausen that had pledged to supply the Swiss army. The wagons were defended by 40 Swiss, who put the horsemen to flight and killed 18 horses and three horsemen. According to the legend they lost only one man, Heini Schuler from Glarus.[71] He fell wounded. His tunic with the Swiss cross had slipped over his head, so he could not be recognized and was killed by his own comrades and buried in Mülhausen. After that the Swiss went on the offensive, they then advanced into the Black Forest and took the town of Bonndorf. Then they threatened the Abbey of St. Blasien whose Prince-Abbot Christoph von Greuth bought himself free with a large ransom (supposedly 1,500 guilders).

Spurred on by the success of the Bernese in Sundgau, the other Swiss advanced on the Habsburg's town of Waldshut and besieged it in the summer of 1468 (the siege began on 29 July).[72] The Bernese, Freiburgers and Solothurners joined them but were unable to capture the town that was held by Bilgeri von Heudorf and Wernher von Schinen. It was the Swiss' own fault: despite the

---

65 The High Rhine (German: *Hochrhein*) is the name used for the part of the Rhine that flows westbound from Lake Constance to Basel.

66 This Swiss city and the surrounding Canton are now generally known by the French name Fribourg but also by its German name Freiburg (also called Freiburg im Üchtland or Uechland) to distinguish it from Freiburg im Breisgau in Germany.

67 Mülhausen or Muelhausen, now French Mulhouse, is a city and commune in eastern France, close to the Swiss and German borders. It was part of the southern Alsatian county of Sundgau in the Holy Roman Empire. From 1354 to 1515, Mulhouse was part of the Décapole, an association of ten Free Imperial Cities in Alsace. The city joined the Swiss Confederation as an associate in 1515 and was therefore not annexed by France in the Peace of Westphalia in 1648 like the rest of the Sundgau. An enclave in Alsace, it was a free and independent Calvinist republic, known as Stadtrepublik Mülhausen, associated with the Swiss Confederation until, after a vote by its citizens on 4 January 1798, it became a part of France in the Treaty of Mulhouse signed on 28 January 1798, during the Directory period of the French Revolution. Source: Wikipedia. For more on Sundgau, see the footnote below.

68 See Seehase, Hagen and Ollesch, Detlef, *Kurfürst Frledrlch der Siegreiche von der Pfalz (1425-1476)* (Petersberg: Imhof Verlag, 2013, pp. 76-79. In Kauzner, Matthias, "*Die Gerichtsordnung des Stadtgerichts der Stadt Mülhausen im Elsaß aus dem 15. Jahrhundert (1424 bis 1484)*", in Forum Historiae Iuris (https://forhistiur.de/en/2001-02-kauzner/?l=de) it indicates the so-called "*Sechs-Plappert-Krieg*" originated in 1462. A miller's servant, Hermann Klee, demanded six "*Plaphart*" (in Basel dialect "*Plappert*", being a 'thick-penny') from his former master for back pay. When the city rejected the complaint, some nobles took up Klee's cause and threatened the city. The city concluded an alliance with Bern and Solothurn in 1466 to last for twenty-five years. Only after many years of continuing conflict were the nobles defeated.

69 Sundgau (French pronunciation: [sunˈgo], German: [ˈzʊntgaʊ]) is a geographical territory in the southern Alsace region (Haut Rhin and Belfort), on the eastern edge of France. The name is derived from Alemannic German "*Sunt-gowe*" ("South shire"), denoting an Alemannic county in the Old High German period. The principal city and historical capital is Altkirch. Source: Wikipedia.

70 Thann in Alsace is now a commune in the northeastern French department of Haut-Rhin (High Rhine), in Grand Est.

71 Aegidius Tschudi reported about this in his *Chronicon Helveticum*.

72 See Hansjakob, Heinrich, *Der Waldshuter Krieg vom Jahre 1468* (Waldshut: Heinrich Zimmermann, 1866), p. 30.

On the march
Photo: Susan Sümer

Duke Sigismund mortgages the Alsace to Charles the Bold
from Diebold Schilling's Chronicle

Waldshut guilds' courageous defense the town would have definitely fallen if it had not been for the disunity in the Swiss besiegers' army about how to conduct further operations. Some of the Swiss cantons were eager to have the Black Forest communities join the federation, or at least they strove for good relations with them. And that precisely must have caused worries for Duke Sigismund. Sigismund's influential council feared the loss of the Forest communities to the Swiss Confederation. The Duke did not have enough power to relieve the city on his own: a group of hired Bohemian mercenaries were located somewhat north of Waldshut in the Black Forest, but they did not attack.

Now Duke Sigismund began peace negotiations with the Swiss. A peace treaty (the so-called "*Waldshuter Richtung*"), mediated by the Castle Count (*Burggraf*) of Nuremberg and other representatives of the nobles, went into effect on 27 August 1468. It was agreed in the treaty that Sigismund had to pay the Swiss a transfer fee of 10,000 Rhenish guilders and surrender Waldshut and the Black Forest as collateral. On 26 May 1469, Emperor Fredrick III, a cousin of Duke Sigismund, declared the treaty as invalid and on 31 August issued an Imperial declaration outlawing the Swiss Confederation, but it had no further effect. But something else had fatal consequences.

Sigismund of Austria, due to his extravagant spending on his court, could not raise the 10,000 guilders. Therefore, in 1469 he turned to King Louis XI of France who brushed him off, so he appealed to Charles the Bold for help. The latter had his counselors Guillaume de Rochefort and Guillaume de la Baume pay the Swiss the 10,000 guilders Sigismund owed them. Additionally, he concluded the Treaty of Omer with Sigismund on 5 September 1469. Charles paid the Tyrolean 50,000 guilders and in exchange received the County of Pfirt (French: Ferrette), the rural County of Upper Alsace, the Black Forest, the four Forest Cities on the Rhine plus Breisach[73] as liens. Furthermore, he obligated Sigismund to side with him against the Swiss.

---

73 German names: *Grafschaft Pfirt, Landgrafschaft Oberelsass, Schwarzwald, Waldstaedte am Rhein* and *Breisach.*

BURGUNDIAN DOMINATION ON THE UPPER RHINE

Thus, the city of Bern got a dangerous neighbor to its north that aroused its concerns: its Habsburg archenemy had allied himself with the powerful Duke of Burgundy. Even though Charles the Bold assured the Swiss it was a purely defensive alliance, the Burgundian-Swiss relations became clouded. Duke Sigismund hoped that Charles would stand by him militarily, but even though in 1472 Pope Sixtus IV urged the Burgundian Duke to go to war with the Swiss, Charles did not want to get involved.

French King Louis XI promised the Swiss help. In 1470, Niklaus von Diesbach, the Bern mayor (*Schultheiss*), who was receiving a lucrative pension from King Louis, negotiated a treaty with him. In it, the two parties promised to not help Charles the Bold if he attacked the other party.

Three years later the cantons issued a prohibition to their populations forbidding them to perform military (mercenary) services for Burgundy. Moreover, the tensions between Burgundy and the Swiss increased because of the large transits of mercenaries from Lombardy, Venice and Naples hired by Charles the Bold via the Confederation.

Then the Margrave Rudolf IV of Hachberg-Sausenberg, in the name of the Burgundian Duke, officially took over the liened lands as Burgundian domains. Charles then named a far lower ranking noble as the mayor of Thann, and then gave him an even more important post.

This Burgundian Steward (*Landvogt*) of the lien-lands, Peter von Hagenbach,[74] quickly got into conflict with the Imperial City of Strassburg. He had been the Steward by the grace of the Duke since 20 September 1469. Only a few months later he wrote an arrogant letter to the Strassburg Council telling them to await the choice of a new "*Ammeister*" (mayor). Duke Charles would name a new one. In 1470 Hagenbach had Burgundian troops storm the Ortenberg Castle whose (co-) owners, the Strassburg Muellenheim family, were noted for conducting plundering raids. The castle controlled the entrance to the Weiler Valley (*Weilertal*), an important route through the Vosges Mountains. In the summer of 1470, Philipp Wetzel *zu* (of) Ortenburg and Diebold von Gippich had carried off three Burgundian merchants to the castle and demanded a ransom. The Burgundian Duke therefore thought he had a rightful title to the castle. Hagenbach gathered a mighty force of about 5,000 men and put them under the command of Jean II de Neuchâtel-Montaigu. The castle's small garrison, two captains, five "*Reisige*" (men-at-arms), and six to eight day-workers surrendered very quickly. On 21 November 1470 the Burgundians were lords of the castle.

Around this time, in order to maintain good relations with the Palatine Electoral Prince (*Pfälzer Kurfürst*) Friedrich – called Friedrich the Victorious (*der Siegreiche*), Charles the Bold instructed Hagenbach to recall all Burgundian vassals in the service of Duke Ludwig of Pfalz-Zweibrücken-Veldenz who was often in conflict with the Palatine Electoral Prince.[75]

At the end of August 1472 Duke Sigismund was negotiating with Swiss representatives in Constance, but then received a delegation from the Burgundian Duke with Hagenbach at its head. Sigismund tasked the knight Hermann von Eptingen to enquire in Basel and Strassburg whether he could get enough money to pay off the lien. A short time later, Sigismund and Hagenbach met in Basel. The city council objected to Hagenbach about the prohibition on selling provisions to Basel that he had issued on 9 July, and the council got an arrogant reply from him.

In the beginning of 1473 the Steward (*Landvogt*), Hagenbach, demanded that Mülhausen to be put under Burgundian protection. He referred to the city as "a weed in a rose garden" which did not please the Mülhausen population, and they and the other Imperial Cities put out feelers to the Swiss Confederation.

Ortenberg Castle
Photo: Marko Tjemmes

To Upper Alsace's self-assured nobles, Hagenbach appeared to be an upstart. He came from a not very well-to-do noble family from the Sundgau. His father, Anton von Hagenbach, was once the mayor of Thann; his mother

---

74 See Brauer-Gramm, *Hildburg, Der Landvogt Peter von Hagenbach, Die burgundische Herrschaft am Oberrhein 1469-1474* (Goettingen: Musterschmidt-Verlag, 2001).

75 The Palatine Electoral Prince got his revenge in that he held out the prospect to Charles the Bold of getting 300 horsemen for a possible campaign against France.

was a Burgundian noblewoman. However, initially Hagenbach was not unwelcomed by the Upper Alsatian nobles. Anyway, he had named a local man, Hans Bernhard von Gilgenberg-Ramstein[76] as his deputy. Furthermore, Gilgenberg occupied the office of the president of Ensisheim's government that – as under Habsburg rule – consisted of local nobles. And Hagenbach's manner toward the Imperial Cities pleased many lords from Upper Alsace.

On 28 March 1473 the Steward introduced an extremely unpopular users' tax ("The Bad Penny" – "*Der Böse Pfennig*").[77] What especially caused annoyance was the fact that he had not consulted with the estates about the tax. In the course of that year the Milanese envoy Gabriele Morosini was staying in Basel, and he warned the city council that the Burgundian Duke had some plans against the city.

At the end of 1473 Charles the Bold along with 4,000 soldiers – mostly from Lombardy - visited his new province and took lodgings in Pfirt. Colmar had shut its gates to the Burgundian Duke and the country folk had fled to the fortified town. Charles' field commander, Wilhelm Herter von Hertneck[78] also arrived at the Burgundian camp at Pfirt. He brought with him 800 German mercenaries from the Black Forest.

At the beginning of 1474 Charles the Bold wanted to begin an attack on Mülhausen, against which he had no rights at all. On 3 January he assembled a large army. In the meantime, the city and the Bishop of Strassburg, the Alsatian Imperial Cities of the *Dekapolis*[79] and the Electoral Palatine (*Kurpfalz*) had united against Burgundy. But their help definitely would have come too late, but very bad storms delayed the Burgundians' planned attack on Mülhausen. In Basel, people worried, not without cause, that they were the actual objective of the Burgundian greediness. Furthermore, the most important bridge over the Rhine in the region was in Basel. On 12 January 1474 Duke Charles left the Sundgau again. His governor, Hagenbach, prohibited the residents of the lien-lands from conducting trade in grains with the Upper Alsatian Imperial Cities, which created new discontent. The discord became so loud and clear that the *Landvogt* thought Alsatian Thann had become too dangerous as his residence. He had had four townsmen hanged there and the citizenry became angry. But Hagenbach had also grossly provoked the residents of Breisach. In 1474 he disbanded the guilds and even forbade them from visiting their pubs. Then he dismissed the city council and named two new mayors.

In 1474 Duke Sigismund urged Charles anew to go to war against the Swiss Confederation; however, Charles again refused. When it was finally clear to Sigismund that the Duke of Burgundy would not engage in his plans against the Swiss, he radically changed course and tried to ally with the Swiss Confederation.

Initially they joined the important alliance with the "Lower Union' ("*Niedere Vereinigung*"), an alliance of the Imperial Cities of Basel, Colmar, Schlettstadt[80] and Strassburg, but then thanks to the support of Louis XI, the "Eternal Direction" ("*Ewige Richtung*") treaty with Duke Sigismund ensued, concluded on 30 March 1474. Decisively, the Bishop of Constance, Hermann von Breitenlandenberg, who in 1466 had mediated between the Swiss and the Tyrolean Duke, helped shape the treaty. In the "*Ewige Richtung*" agreement, Sigismund renounced all his territorial claims in the Swiss Confederation and recognized them as being independent from Habsburg rule. The Swiss in return pledged to never again touch the Habsburg lands on the other side of the border.

Then Sigismund told Duke Charles he was terminating the treaty on the lien-lands. The Alsatian cities had raised 80,000 guilders to pay off the lien. But Charles refused to accept the termination of the Treaty of St. Omer, because he had invested another 170,000 guilders in the leased lands.[81] But Sigismund could not give him that money. Indeed, the wheels of history had already turned further.

---

[76] Hans Bernhard von Gilgenberg was the illegitimate son of the Baron (*Freiherr*) Rudolf von Ramstein whose ancestral home was in the vicinity of Solothurn. As the illegitimate son he was not entitled to his father's title, therefore he only called himself "von Gilgenberg". In 1474 he became the Steward of the Forest (*Waldvogt*) of the County (*Grafschaft*) of Hauenstein in the southern Black Forest.

[77] At this time the tax burden was also increasing in the other Burgundian territories.

[78] In 1468 he had been was named by Duke Sigismund as the Steward of Waldshut and had gone into the Duke's service on his own initiative.

[79] The "*Zehnstädtebund*" or "Ten City Alliance" – but Strassburg, the largest and most influential Imperial City in Alsace, was not a member.

[80] Schlettstadt is now known by its French name Sélestat.

[81] In the previous years, Duke Sigismund himself had already leased parts of the region to other nobles and cities. The Duke of Burgundy had gradually had to take over these lease costs in order to get control over these places, for example, over Thann that was mortgaged to Heinrich Reich von Reichenstein.

Burgundian noble
Photo: Susan Süme

Burgundian soldier
Photo: Susan Sümer

Camp scene
Photo: Susan Sümer

THE UPRISING AGAINST CHARLES THE BOLD'S STEWARD

The residents of the leased lands, who were tired of the tax burdens and the Burgundian Steward's continuous new humiliations, revolted. The first uprisings occurred in Thann, then the citizens of Ensisheim refused to allow Hagenbach's mercenaries from Picardy to transit. Hagenbach's German mercenaries in Breisach were becoming unruly because they had not received their pay. So they in turn could no longer pay their innkeepers. According to a story passed down, Hagenbach responded to the soldiers' complaints with a drastic recommendation: "Everyone should beat his innkeeper to death."[82] When the Picardians arrived in Breisach, Hagenbach ordered the German troops to immediately to vacate their quarters in order to make room for those from Picardy. The German mercenaries' officers, under the leadership of Friedrich Kappler, went to Hagenbach and handed in their resignations. Hagenbach, who no longer trusted the German mercenaries, ordered them together with the town's citizens to dig a moat around the town so as to get them out of the town. In order to do this work, they would have had to remove their armor, and would then be vulnerable to attack by the troops from Picardy. Captain Vögelin, who was from Breisach, was immediately dismissed. But he was still the informal leader of the German mercenaries and gave a counter-order. Then Breisach's citizens risked starting an uprising, and Hagenbach's German mercenaries – still another 200 men – under the command of their ex-captain (and actual leader) Vögelin, changed sides. Peter von Hagenbach was arrested on Easter Sunday, 11 April 1474. Richard von Zessingen took him captive and had him led to the tower in chains. The same happened to Wernher von Pforr, whom Hagenbach had appointed the mayor. Hagenbach was handed over to the Lower Union (*Niedere Vereinigung*). He was put in irons and guarded by three especially large men-at-arms. Meanwhile, Duke Sigismund ordered torture instruments be brought from Basel.

The Lombard mercenaries who had been driven out of Breisach sent a delegation to Breisach's citizenry, distanced themselves from Hagenbach, and asked to get their property back. Thereupon they got their possessions and withdrew. However, some Lombards plundered the village of Reiningen, and killed the proprietor of the inn along with his son. The village cleric, who tried to intervene, was wounded. Then the farmers rose up and attacked the mercenary troop. Those who were not killed fled in the direction of Belfort. The remaining Burgundian positions within the Habsburg lands quickly fell. Only the castle of Thann remained in their hands. But when the cities' levies, reinforced with Habsburg regular troops, moved against the castle, the Burgundian commander, Anton von Münsterol, requested his troops be allowed to leave peacefully; his request was granted on 1 May 1474. In the meanwhile, Hagenbach was put before a court for trial. The former Steward was repeatedly subjected to "mortifying interrogation" ("*peinlichen Verhör*"), i.e., torture. He was brought before the court on a cart because he was no longer able to walk as a result of the torture. The court, under the presidency of Thomas Schütz von Ensisheim, accused Hagenbach of the following crimes:

Judicial murder of four citizens of Thann,
Breaking of the oath to abide by the laws of Breisach,
Conspiracy to murder citizens of Breisach, and
Rape of women and virgins, including nuns.[83]

Among the 26 members of the court, two came from Bern and two from Solothurn; the others were from Alsatian and Upper Rhine towns. Hagenbach claimed to have only been following orders; they answered that a lord could not order such infamous actions and no servant was permitted to carry out such orders. The court sentenced Hagenbach to death. Burgundian Duke Charles attempted to intervene in writing with Duke Sigismund, but without success.

On 9 May 1474 about four o'clock in the morning, Peter von Hagenbach was executed in Breisach: according to traditional precedent, Hagenbach was symbolically expelled from knighthood by Duke Sigismund's Chief of Heraldry, Caspar Hurter, and was beheaded by the executioner of Colmar. According to legend, eight executioners argued for the privilege of beheading Hagenbach. Colmar's executioner was physically the smallest, but he understood his profession.

For over 200 years the *Bibliotheque municipale* (municipal library) in Colmar maintained a mummified head that was attributed to Peter von Hagenbach, but which probably was untrue. Therefore, the gruesome artifact bore the curious designation as the "Pseudo-head [*Pseudokopf*] of Peter von Hagenbach". One had chosen the more honorable execution variant of beheading in order not to provoke Charles the Bold any further. After all, Hagenbach belonged to the close circle of advisors trusted by the otherwise very suspicious Duke. The Chancellor Guillaume Hugonet, Guy de Brimeau, Antoine Haneron and the *Pronotar* Guillaume de Clugny also belonged to this circle.[84] After Hagenbach had played an important role in exposing a plot to murder Charles in 1461, he was named

---

82 Quoted in Vulpinus, Theodor, *Ritter Friedrich Kappler, Ein Elsässischer Feldhauptmann aus dem 15. Jahrhundert* (Strassburg: Ed. Heitz, 1896), p. 30.

83 See Heller, Kevin Jon and Simpson, Gerry (Ed.), *The Hidden Histories of War Crime Trials* (Oxford: Oxford University Press, 2013), p. 33.

84 See Ehm-Schnocks, Petra, *Burgund und das Reich* (Munich: Oldenbourg, 2002), p. 147. A "*pronotar*", from the Latin "*ponotarius*", was the first chairman of a princely chancellery (http://www.enzyklo.de/Begriff/Protonotar).

as the head of the court. It was clear to everyone involved that the Burgundian Duke would not simply accept such a loss like Hagenbach's execution. Initially Hans Bernhard von Gilgenberg succeeded Hagenbach as the Burgundian steward in the land. But that had no practical effect because the Burgundian rule there had collapsed – so, for example, the Strassburgers had retaken the castle of Ortenburg on 19 April 1474.[85]

Trial of Peter von Hagenbach
from Diebold Schilling's Chronicle

After Hagenbach's death, the Alsatians declared themselves free of Burgundian rule and recognized Duke Sigismund as their new (old) liege. A delegation from Breisach had informed the Burgundian Duke about Hagenbach's capture; on 17 April Chief of Heraldry Caspar Hurter appeared and ceremoniously announced the dismissal of the *Pfandschaftsvertrag*.[86] On 22 April, Duke Charles still answered in a conciliatory tone. That changed drastically after Hagenbach's death.

Duke Charles attempted to secure a position in Alsace by promising 10,000 guilders to a group of Alsatian nobles around Jakob von Hohenstein if they would hand over some castles and towns in Alsace. The Bishop of Strassburg learned about the plan. The Strassburgers were able to capture the important castle Girbaden ("Chateau Guirbaden"), the main base of the conspirators and take them prisoner in a surprise attack.

Duke Charles of Burgundy did not just passively watch the developments in the leased lands and took the initiative even before Hagenbach's beheading: the Parliament of High Burgundy declared the County of Mömpelgard (French: Montbéliard) as a Burgundian fiefdom and Duke Charles claimed it as his. The Imperial Chancellery very rapidly issued an urgent announcement that Mömpelgard was an Imperial fiefdom. But this did not especially impress the Burgundian Duke, and he took an armed force to Mömpelgard that was the gateway to Alsace. The claim that he believed he had on the county was less than thin: according to the 12 July 1473 Treaty of Urach, all of the properties of the counts of Wurttemberg on the left [west] of the Rhine had been given to the 24-year old Count Heinrich von Wurttemberg.[87] Because the dominions of Granges, Clerval and Passavant belonging to Mömpelgard were Burgundian fiefs, Duke Charles had had to concur with the treaty.

Count Heinrich von Wurttemberg went to the Burgundian Duke's area of control with only a small retinue – we don't know why to this day – and was promptly taken prisoner. Even though the Count assured that he wanted to remain neutral in the conflict between Burgundy and the Lower Union, the Duke treated him as an enemy. He was pressured into giving a written order that all Wurttemberg garrisons in Mömpelgard were to open their gates to the Burgundian forces commanded by Olivier de Marche. The commander of Mömpelgard's town and castle, Herr Marquard von Stein,[88] refused to carry out the coerced order. Then Heinrich von Wurttemberg was brought before the town, was threatened with execution if Mömpelgard's commander continued to be so obstinate. The executioner had already raised his sword when Marquard von Stein shouted that they should not capitulate even if they murdered the Count. In reaction, the vile charade was halted, the poor Count was led away, and he remained in Burgundian captivity in Boulogne and Maastricht until 1477. The County of Mömpelgard, or at least those parts occupied by the Burgundians, were handed over to Stephan von Hagenbach, the younger brother of the executed steward, who was named as governor by the Burgundian Duke.

---

85 Thereafter Gilgenberg served as the commander of the mercenaries from Picardy at the siege of Neuss. During the siege there, on 9 October 1474, he was struck and killed by a cannonball.

86 This was a so-called "pledge treaty" regarding Duke Sigismund's control of Alsace. "In areas of very uncertain jurisdiction, contracts like [Italian] *'accomandigia'* or the German *'Pfandschaft'* defined the local framework of justice and fiscality, enabling both to flourish by determining who held what rights, over whom and from whom…" Watts, John, *The Making of Polities: Europe, 1300-1500* (Cambridge: Cambridge University Press, 2009), p. 249.

87 Born 7 September 1448 in Stuttgart, died 15 April 1519 in the Hohenurach castle.

88 In many depictions the castle's commander is named as Jakob von Stein who was his cousin.

The members of the Lower Union were completely aware that something was brewing. At a meeting in Ensisheim, at the suggestion of Peter von Mörsberg – he was Marquard von Stein's father-in-law - it was agreed to the effect to position a few hundred men-at-arms in especially critical towns along the route to Burgundy. Additionally, a message was sent to the Electoral Prince of the Palatine (*Kurfürst von der Pfalz*) asking him to serve as a negotiator.

Wilhelm and Friedrich Kappler, who with a force of Alsatian knights who had formerly been in Hagenbach's service, showed themselves to be not ready at all to compromise and attacked into the Free County of Burgundy on 24 June, allegedly to compensate for their unpaid wages.

A 6,000-man force of Burgundian mercenaries, with Stephan von Hagenbach as a guide knowledgeable about the country, departed on 18 August 1474 and went burning and murdering through the Sundgau. Their commander was Count Heinrich von Neuenburg-Blamont (Henri de Neuchâtel-Blamont).[89] He had six *Ordonnance* companies alone under his command.[90] According to Giovan Pietro Panigarola, the Milanese emissary to Duke Charles, the Count was the Duke's representative and deputy on the border with the "Germans" ("*Deutschen*"). The Burgundians could not take Thann, but the devastation that they caused in the surrounding area was indescribable. The contemporary chroniclers outdid one another in their descriptions of the atrocities against the population; the Italian mercenaries appear to have excelled in that. The Burgundians withdrew quickly, and the Lower Union immediately created a border guard of 100 armored men-at-arms under Wernher von Schinen. One week later, the Lower Union, which had named Wilhelm Herter von Hertneck as the commander in chief of their forces, began a counteroffensive. The Sundgau nobles' levies were joined by units from the Alsatian Imperial cities, and then by 600 mercenaries in Basel's service and 400 fighters selected from the Basel guilds.[91] But the first battle went badly for the allies. A levy of Sundgau peasants (300 men from Pfirt) fought a fierce battle with the Count of Neuchâtel-Blamont's horsemen in which the peasants were defeated. The peasantry was mostly armed with crossbows and hand-cannon and foolishly left a defensive position. In heavy rain, their crossbow strings became wet and their guns' matches were extinguished. So, they were powerless against the attacking Burgundian horsemen's edged weapons. Eighty-nine peasants were killed and 100 were taken prisoner.

Duke Charles was in the meantime (since 29 June 1474) busy with the siege of Neuss. He had gotten involved in the "Cologne Bishopric's Feud" ("*Kölner Stiftsfehde*"), the struggle for the bishop's seat. In doing so, he provoked Emperor Friedrich II and the Imperial Cities to declare war on him. The Emperor also asked the Swiss to send forces to relieve Neuss. A Swiss delegation met with the Emperor in Andernach and told him that the Swiss Confederation would certainly fight against the Burgundian Duke but preferably in the south, in the area near Switzerland. In any case, Basel sent about 200 men[92] under the command of Veltin von Neuenstein.[93] The Prince-Abbot of Saint Gallen, Ulrich Rösch, also sent a small contingent.

Under Diesbach's chairmanship, the Swiss Confederation had concluded an alliance treaty with France. Actually, King Louis wanted to lull the Swiss into a sense of security and goad them into a war with Charles the Bold. In the treaty it was agreed that Louis XI would rush to the aid of the Swiss should Duke Charles attack them. In the event that he did not personally engage in the war, he promised to pay compensation in the amount of 20,000 guilders and 20,000 francs per quarter for the duration of the war. Additionally, the French king pledged to pay the eight cantons as well as Freiburg (Fribourg) and Solothurn 2,000 francs per year until his death, and four and one-half guilders per man per year for the recruiting of Swiss mercenaries. All the parties, except for one that had a non-aggression agreement with the Burgundians, signed the treaty.

King Louis went further: he also promised to give Duke Sigismund, who was chronically short of money, an annuity of 10,000 francs for which the latter pledged to renounce any ties with Charles the Bold and to make his forces available to the French king against Burgundy.

Charles also used money as a means of persuasion. He sent his emissary Symon de Cleron several hundred Rhenish guilders that he was to disperse among certain German lords and knights so they would not participate in campaigns against Burgundy.

---

89 He was the brother of Claude de Neuchâtel, Sire du Fay. On Duke Charles' orders, he had given over his command to his brother Henri. See Witte, Heinrich, *"Zur Geschichte der Burgunderkriege"*, in *Zeitschrift für die Geschichte des Oberrheins* (Freiburg im Breisgau: Kohlhammer, 1891), pp. 2-81, here p. 45.

90 It was the 9th Ordonnance Company (Hagenbach's old command) with 100 "Lances" and 300 bowmen, and the 4th, 12th, 16th and 18th the *Ordonnance* Companies.

91 They were commanded by the Chief Guild Master (*Oberzunftmeister*) Heinrich Iselin.

92 The troops were uniformly dressed in blue and red and had been organized by Meinrad Schütz from Waldshut.

93 In 1475 Basel sent 100 men under Veltin von Neuenstein (in some sources he is called Valentin von Neuenstein). The troops arrived too late to fight against the Burgundians. Neuenstein and his people busied themselves with plundering the vicinity and thus were no threat to the Burgundians.

Close combat
Photo: Susan Sümer

Attacking an earthwork
Photo: Susan Sümer

THE SWISS CONFEDERATION'S FIRST ATTACKS ON BURGUNDY

As a result of the French assurances and payments, on 25 October 1474, Bern declared war on Burgundy in the name of the Swiss Confederation. Two days later, the Bernese invaded Burgundy's ally Savoy and captured the domain of Erlach.[94] Two days after that, the Swiss together with Outer Austrians[95] and the Alsatians departed with 18,000 men toward Héricourt and besieged that small town that likewise belonged to Charles' ally, the lord of Neuchâtel-Blamont. But initially the siege was unsuccessful and on 13 November a Burgundian relief force arrived. It had a total of almost 12,000 men. It was under the command of Count Henri de Neuchâtel-Blamont, who held the rank of a Marshal of Burgundy. The Burgundian Grand Marshal Jacques de Romont with a 5,000 man Italian force also joined Blamont's forces. Exactly what occurred was never passed down historically. Supposedly Neuchâtel-Blamont found out how strong and battle-ready the opposing army was and withdrew his forces. The Allies pursued him closely and caught up with the Burgundians in a plain between Chatebier and Chenebier. The Burgundians arrayed themselves for battle between a pond and a thicket and thought by doing so they would be safe from attack on their flanks.

The main body of the Swiss army made a frontal advance against the Burgundians and thus drew their full attention, while a force of Bernese and Lucerners took a trail through the woods. All of a sudden that force emerged from the woods that covered the Burgundian left flank and attacked the enemy. The attack startled the Burgundians sufficiently that the battle was decided within a few minutes. The dreaded Burgundian cavalry did nothing against the Alsatian cavalry and fled.

Two thousand Burgundians lay dead on the battlefield.[96] The Swiss claimed to have only suffered 70 dead. The same day, the Bishop of Basel's men captured the Franquemont castle whose Burgundian garrison had put up resistance for three long days.[97] On 17 November the town of Héricourt also surrendered to the besiegers. Prisoners who had been captured after the battle were later freed in exchange for ransoms. Sixty "Lombards" (i.e., probably the Duke's Italian mercenaries) were held captive in Basel, 18 of them were charged with all sorts of crimes and on Christmas Eve of 1474 in Basel they were burned at the stake as heretics.[98]

Due to wintery storms after taking Héricourt, the Allied army had gone home but left Friedrich Kappler as commandant there with 200 horsemen and an equal number of footsoldiers. When on 6 December 1474 a Burgundian assault force of 300 men appeared, Kappler's troops chased them off and took ten prisoners. At the end of March 1475, the Burgundians appeared again, but Kappler drove them off once more.

On 3 January 1475, the Bernese had already stormed Illingen (Fr.: Illens), where Guillaume de la Baume, the Duke of Burgundy's Counselor, was building an elegant palace; the construction ended abruptly.

The Swiss now urged King Louis again to join the war, however he delayed and instead he sent the first annuity to Bern to calm their feelings. At a council of war, representatives of the Lower Union wanted to advance to Dijon in the heart of Burgundy, but the Swiss rejected the proposal. In any case, small bands of Swiss fighters independently pushed through the Sundgau into Burgundian territory as far as Faucogney to loot and "thus drive away the wintertime".[99] In 1475 a 1,300-man group of irregulars from Bern, Lucerne and Solothurn attacked the Free County of Pontarlier and took the town and palace, however they were soon surrounded by a 7,000-man, impressive army under Louis de Chalon.[100] Diesbach rushed with 3,000 men from Solothurn, Biel, Freiburg and Bern to their aid, but the surrounded troops were able to break out of Pontarlier on their own together with all their booty. Marshal Louis de Chalon's army repeatedly attacked Diesbach's small force, but he was able to face up to the Burgundians each time. On the way back, Diesbach got another 2,000 reinforcements including 500 from Basel. The Council of Basel had recognized that this operation by the irregulars could become a larger campaign and pledged Bern its support.

---

94 They belonged to the Burgundian fiefs of the de Chalon family.

95 The Austrian forelands, sometimes called Outer Austria, Further Austria, or Anterior Austria (*Vorderösterreich*) was the collective name for the early possessions of the House of Habsburg in the former Swabian stem duchy of southwestern Germany, including territories in the Alsace region west of the Rhine and in Vorarlberg.

96 According to one description, the Burgundians only lost 500 men. Two flags and two stone-firing cannon fell into the victors' hands. See Vulpinus, Theodor, *Ritter Friedrich Kappler, Ein Elsässischer Feldhauptmann aus dem 15. Jahrhundert* (Strassburg: Ed. Heitz, 1896), p. 51.

97 The Burgundians were allowed to leave peacefully. See *La Société Générale d'Histoire Suisse (Ed.): Indicateur d'HIstoire Suisse* (Solothurn 1877), p. 208.

98 See Vaughan, Richard, *Charles the Bold, The Last Valois Duke of Burgundy* (London and New York: Boydell Press, 1973), p. 296.

99 In medieval Swiss-German dialect *"damit die zyt des winters zu vertriben"*, quoted from Wackernagel, Rudolf, *Geschichte der Stadt Basel. Zweiten Bandes erster Teil* (Basel: Helbing & Lichtenhahn, 1911), p. 81.

100 See Wieland, Johannes, *Geschichte der Kriegsbegebenheiten in Helvetien und Rhätien als Handbuch zum Militärunterricht für Schweizeroffiziere aller Waffen, Band 1* (Basel: Schweighauser'schen Buchhandlung, 1827).

CAMPAIGN OF CONQUEST IN WAADT (VAUD)

Very encouraged by the progress of the Lower Union's and the Empire's war against Burgundy, the notorious peace-breaker Count Wilhelm I von der Marc (Guillaume de la Marck)[101] went from Cologne, where he had spent the winter of 1474-75, to his old area of operations, the Ardennes. Starting in April 1475 he carried out attacks against Burgundian properties there. Although he was helped by Raes van Heers, the leader of the Liégeois resistance against Charles the Bold at that time, he had little success. The population of the Malmendy region did in fact support the uprising, but Charles' governor in the Netherlands, Guy de Brimeu, Sire de Humbercourt, quickly put it down.

On 9 May 1475, Duke René II (or Renatus II) of Lorraine, completely overestimating his possibilities, sent a declaration of war to the Burgundian Duke who was camped before besieged Neuss.[102] According to the legend, the Duke of Lorraine's herald handed over a blood-smeared gauntlet as a symbol of the declaration of hostilities.[103] Duke Charles happily accepted this declaration of war not only because it agreed with his concepts of chivalry, but also because it came at just the right time for his strategic plans. In any case he had no time to turn against Lorraine just then. Lorraine's military actions against the Burgundians in Luxembourg were, however, not crowned with great success. Duke René II had ensured the neutrality of the Imperial City of Metz through a treaty, had allied French troops under the command of George Georges de La Trémoille, Sire de Craon, had taken Damville after days of siege, and on 7 June Lorraine troops destroyed the castle at Pierrefort. Not much else was accomplished, also because de La Trémoille refrained from further offensive actions at the command of his king.

The Bernese actions had already had different results. Despite any agreements, Diesbach took his army into northern Waadt[104] in order to secure the northern passes in the Jura Mountains against Burgundy, to thereby cut off Savoy from Burgundy, and to provoke a war.

Grandson and Echallens surrendered. The town of Orbe resisted, was taken by storm and its garrison was slaughtered mercilessly. The defenders in Jougne were also killed. Afterward, Diesbach had his forces return home.

In the meantime, the Swiss Assembly, "die Tagsatzung,[105] criticized Diesbach's independent action and decided for the timebeing to no longer support Bern militarily. The other Swiss Confederation members feared the Bernese were becoming too strong and gaining too much power and their excellent relationship with the French crown could result in too stong a position. Meanwhile, the French King used the opportunity and had his army invade northern Burgundian territories, and some towns along the Somme River – Montdidier, Roye and Corbie – were captured by the French.

On 19 June 1475 the Lower Union in Ensisheim decided on a campaign against Burgundy with the objective of taking Blamont. Because a long campaign was expected, Basel decided instead of participating with selected men, to employ mercenaries instead. Basel had Captain Heini Breitschedel recruit peasants from within the Confederation, mostly in Lucerne. In addition to mercenaries from the city there were also ones raised in the countryside. Sixty men-at-arms from Basel joined the 600-man Lucerne force. The troops had a large cannon ("*Hauptbüchse*") and a few cannon of smaller calibers.

Charles the Bold noted this looming threat for the Free County of Burgundy and asked the Duke of Milan for military assistance. According to the Treaty of Moncalieri[106] both sides were mutually required to send 400 "*lances*".[107] And now Charles requested them.

In July 1475 Diesbach moved with his forces into Alsace to suppport the Lower Union and Duke Sigismund. L'Isle-sur-le-Doubs was captured on 19 July 1475, after the city's fall all the Burgundian soldiers and all the male inhabitants were killed, only women, children, the elderly and clergy were spared. The churches were not allowed to be plundered. An Austrian footsoldier stole a chalace from a church and was therefore handed over to an executioner. Because the executioner angered the malefactor's comrades at the execution they stabbed him to death.

Then Diesbach was struck by the blow from a horse's hoof and was unable to serve as the commander-in-chief. The captains started to quarrel about what to do. Count Oswald von Thierstein wanted to lead the army into Lorraine, the commander of the Swiss preferred to besiege

---

101 He was called the "Wild Boar of the Ardennes" – "*Wilden Eber der Ardennen*".

102 See. Kekewich, Margaret L., *The Good King, René of Anjou and Fifteenth Century Europe* (Basingstoke: Palgrave Macmillan, 2008), p. 239.

103 See Köllner, Friedrich, *Geschichte des vormaligen Nassau-Sarbrück´schen Landes und seiner Regenten, 1. Band* (Saarbrücken: Heinrich Arnold, 1841), p. 225. In other descriptions on 9 May a challenge to a knightly single combat, and the formal declaration of war was first delivered after the Duke of Lorraine had joined the alliance between Kaiser Friedrich III and the French crown on 17 May 1475. See Rodt, Emanuel von, *Die Kriege Karls des Kühnen, Herzogs von Burgund und seiner Erben* (Schaffhausen: C. A. Jenni, 1844), p. 420.

104 The Waadt (in French "Vaud") had belonged to Savoy since the 1263 campaigns of Count Peter II of Savoy.

---

105 "*Die Tagsatzung*" was the term used until 1848 for the gathering of the representatives of the Swiss cantons. The term is derived from "to set a day" "*einen Tag setzen*", by which was meant the agreement on the scheduling of the assembly.

106 The treaty was concluded in 1475.

107 A "Lance" or German "*Lanze*" was a small group of armed men centered on an armored horseman, usually totaling about 3 or 4 men.

DESCRIPTION OF THE STORMING OF A CASTLE BY SWISS FIGHTERS

(Capture of the Les Clées Castle in Vaud)

The Allies turned from Yverdon toward Orbe, which, as we know, had already been in their possession since the spring and had been selected as the rallying point. The Les Clées Castle, which still stood near this town, commanded the way over the Jougne Pass. A handpicked body of 1,000 armored men and archers was sent there, but the little town's garrison set it ablaze and retreated into the castle. The castle rose proudly and boldly on a steep hill; its mighty tower, with interior arches, was surrounded by no fewer than four successive walls with strongly barricaded gates. The castle was justifiably considered one of the most secure far and wide. The Allied captain and men did not delay for a moment. The attackers, equipped with large wooden shields, picks and other demolition tools, advanced to the foot of the hill; the order was given that all should attack from the same side with unified strength and "without looking back" (*"ohne hinter sich zu sehen"*) to doggedly carry out the attack. But the handgunners were assigned a position from which they could effectively engage the battlements and loopholes.

Now the troops began the assault. The four-deep walls were scaled; the defenders gave way and fell back to the sturdy tower; those who penetrated the walls were hot on the heels of the defenders and killed those in the rear in fierce hand-to-hand fighting. The tower, the core of the castle, still had to be stormed. But the frightened defenders cried out for mercy. However, all the ill spirits had been unleashed. The defenders should not be spared execution; the besiegers furiously demanded to storm the tower so they could, with sword in hand, kill the enemy.

However, it appeared that among those in the tower awaiting their fate were two Swiss prisoners; they pleaded with the vengeful besiegers not to sacrifice them. So, it was decided to avoid the assault and spare the garrison for later execution. They wanted to accept their pledge "on the sword" and allow them a period to rest and make confession. The gate opened; inside were still about 70 men who were immediately bound and taken to Orbe and put before a court martial.

That very same evening death sentences were handed down; all the nobles and peasants were to be executed with a sword. But because there was no executioner at the location, they asked whether one of the prisoners wanted to prolong his life by taking up the sword to carry out the execution. It was reported that the German, who was chosen from those who asked for the task, a handsome man with strong limbs, had carried out the bloody work so effectively that it seemed he had done this job before. After five prisoners had received the deadly blow, the judges recognized that darkness was approaching and postponed the rest of the executions until the following day. On the next morning another five heads fell and during the night 19 prisoners had suffocated in the confined tower where they were held. The remainder were given their lives and freedom.

Even though the assault had lasted from morning until evening, the attackers counted not more than four dead and of the sixty wounded, the majority recovered. The castle was put to the torch and its ruins are still visible today; only the small town was rebuilt. The reports were that the plundering of the unlucky inhabitants was bad. The only trophy that fell into the victors' hands was a small Savoyard flag (*"Panner"*) with a white cross on a red field.

(from Frey, Emil, <u>Die Kriegstaten der Schweizer dem Volk erzählt</u>
(Neunburg: F. Zahn, 1904)

Burgundian officer
Photo: Susan Sümer

the castles in the area. The Bishop of Basel (Johannes von Venningen) also wanted to do that. Finally Thierstein departed with the Alsatian cavalry, but instead of going to Lorraine they went to their native Alsace. Immediately a rumor circulated that he did not want to hurt the Count of Neuchâtel-Blamont, to whom he was related by marriage, over money. A mutiny ensued in the contingent from Strassburg, and the men from the County of Lichtenberg simply departed under their captain's leadership.[108]

The County of Blamont was almost completely in the Allies' hands, only the castle of Blamont held out. It was defended by several hundred men under the command of Thiébaud de Blamont, an illegitimate offspring of the Count's house. So a 4,000 man besieging army – Swiss and Alsatian footsoldiers - stood opposed to a well-armed castle with substantial provisions. Therefore only artillery helped. After a heavy bombardment with three large "main cannon" ("*Hauptbüchsen*") and similar counterfire from the castle's cannon, did the besiegers attack. It was led by the knight Hans Thüring von Büttikon and his son-in-law Hans Rudolf von Erlach from Bern. The Strassburg forces were led by Kaspar Barpfennig as their captain. When the attack began with Kaspar Barpfennig along with both his sons as the first men on the storming ladders, it became apparent that the ladders were too short! The besieged troops defended themselves by tossing beehives at the attackers. Then the rumor arose that Antoine de Bourgogne, a half-brother of the Duke,

---

[108] In the Chronicles he is called "Cunrat von Myttelshus".

Murten Castle
Photo: Michael Gauger

was on his way with a 7,000-man relief army. In the meantime, it was in August 1475, Diesbach – he had been taken to the Pruntrut Castle (Fr.: Porrentruy)[109] – died of the plague. Supposedly Thiébaud de Blamont was also struck by the pestilence and this sapped the defenders will to resist. Then a large cannon from Strassburg arrived in the besiegers' camp. After a few salvoes from this cannon, the castle's occupants – still about 400 men – surrendered on 9 August. They were allowed to leave in peace. Blamont Castle, from whose dungeons a few half-starved prisoners were freed, was destroyed. After Blamont, the Allies (without the Strassburg Bishop's people commanded by the Lord of Ochsenstein who had returned to the safety of their home city) captured the castle of Grammont, "killed almost one hundred enemy" ("...*erlegten bey hundert feinde*")"[110] and finally captured it. The remainder of the garrison was allowed to leave, however only dressed in their shirts and with a walking stick in their hands. Valant was also captured. Meanwhile the reinforcements from Bern, led by Nikolaus II von Scharnachthal, arrived in the Allies' camp.

---

109 It was one of the Bishop of Basel's residences.

110 Quoted from Ochs, Peter, *Geschichte der Stadt und Landschaft Basel, Band 4* (Basel: Schweighauser'sche Buchhandlung, 1819), p. 247.

The Allies, under Scharnachtal's leadership, now moved against the Castle of Montjoie, south of Blamont. The lord of the castle, the old knight Dietrich von Frohberg was an ally of the Burgundian Duke. But he then appeared in Scharnachtal's quarters to surrender the castle and to pay homage. Due to his advanced age, it was decided to not have him perform any military service. However, he was obligated to send his sons and his vassals to the Allies' army. That a nobleman, who was Duke Sigismund's vassal but had sided with the Burgundians, got off so lightly had a special reason. Frohberg's family was related by marriage to that of Adrian von Bubenberg.[111] He was related through his (second) wife Jeanne[112] to the influential de la Sarraz family of Waadt, who were officials in Savoy and held command positions in Charles' army.

Although Diesbach was dead, the Bernese decided to wage war across the country of Savoy. They claimed the main reason was that the Duchess Jolanthe of Savoy had allowed Italian mercenary forces into her lands and allowed them transit. The confiscation by the Count of Romont's officials of two wagonloads of animal hides that supposedly had been smuggled through Savoy to Lyon was the vociferously presented excuse for the war. The probable, more significant cause was based on the fact that since Diesbach's campaign a few months earlier, there were still Bernese occupiers located in Orbe, Jougne and Grandson who they wanted to reinforce or at least get them out of there.

On 14 October, the Bernese attacked. They captured Murten, where they stationed a garrison of troops from Freiburg under Niklaus Perrotet.[113] They also took the towns of Cudrefin, Avenches, Payerne and Montagny as well as the La Molière castle. The castles of La Sarraz and Sainte Croix were stormed and their garrisons killed. The sturdy Le Clées castle was not easy to take, the garrison under Pierre de Cossonay defended it bravely but in the end was unsuccessful; it fell on 23 October. The town of Estavayer-le-Lac ("Stäffis am See" in German) under the command of Claude d´Estavayer defended itself courageously against 6,000 Bernese and 300 Freiburgers.[114] On 27 October 1475 the attackers pushed their way into the town, according to legend, after some cowardly town guards roped down from their watchtower and fled. The town was devastated, and all of the male population killed. Many women and children attempting to flee across the lake drowned in their sinking overfilled boats. Wagonloads of booty were taken to Fribourg. Even to contemporaries – who were used to such events - the attack on Estavayer appeared to have exceeded what was allowable. The "bad day of Stäffis" ("der böse Tag von Stäffis") remained in the people's memory for a long time. The Council of Bern felt obliged to call upon its military leaders for restraint.[115] But the commanders ignored thse demands.

Swiss storm a city

The towns of the Waadt were gripped with terror. Lausanne and Geneva paid horrific sums to avoid being plundered. Within two weeks Bern and Freiburg took sixteen towns and 43 castles and devastated the Waadt in a merciless campaign.

A unit of Swiss and Breisgau fighters under the command of Captain Henzi Vögelin seized the Grandson castle, which was held by a Burgundian garrison under Pierre de Joigne.[116]

---

111 See Rodt, Emanuel von, *Die Kriege Karls des Kühnen, Herzogs von Burgund und seiner Erben* (Schaffhausen: Hurter'sche Buchhandlung, 1844), p. 451.
112 Jeanne de la Sarraz was the daughter of Guillaume de la Sarraz.
113 The Savoyard mayor of Murten had been Humbertus de Lavigni, and his Swiss Confederation successor was Jakob Felga, Herr zu Löwenberg.
114 According to legend, the Bernese executioner was killed during the storming of Estavayer, and therefore a prisoner taken in Le Clées was chosen to execute his comrades. But the legend does not fit into the chronology of events.

115 See Delbrück, Hans, *Geschichte der Kriegskunst im Rahmen der politischen Geschichte, Teil 3* (Berlin: Georg Stilke, 1923), p. 638.
116 The men from the Rötteln domain, whose lord was Count Rudolf IV von Hachberg-Sausenberg, could have also taken part in this action. He had "citizen rights" ("*Burgrecht*") in the canton of Bern and at the same time lands in Burgundy. In consideration of his political status, the people from Rötteln were given a captain from Bern.

SECONDARY THEATERS OF WAR IN WALLIS (VALAIS) AND LOTHRINGEN (LORRAINE)

Now the Bernese requested the Wallisers to also attack Savoy. Since September 1475 there had been a treaty of alliance between the city of Bern on one side and on the other the Bishop of Sitten (Walter Supersaxo), the "*Domkapitel*"[117] and the "*Zehnden*".[118]. The Duchy of Savoy had a relatively powerful army to which the Neapolitan Condottiere Coluccio de Grisis[119] was obligated to serve with mercenaries (effective on 6 November 1476). The core of the army was however made up of mounted nobles and a few companies organized on the French model of "*franc-archers*".[120] Since 1463, Rudolf Asperlin, one of the wealthiest and most powerful men of Wallis, had lived in Savoy under the protection of the local duke (then duchess). Due to arguments with the Bishop of Sitten over properties, he had bowed to them (the so-called "*Asperlinhandel*"). And a trade embargo had been in place in Savoy against Wallis since 1473. At the request of the Bernese, Wallis attacked Savoy, but their attack on the fortified town of Conthey remained unsuccessful. The town was skillfully defended by troops of the Administrator of the Bishopric of Geneva, Jean-Louis of Savoy.[121]

Then Duchess Jolanthe marched to Conthey with 10,000 reinforcements and then on 13 November 1475 it came to a battle between the Savoyards and the 3,000 to 4,000 Wallisers under the command of the *Junker* (young nobleman) Johann am Hengart, the leader of the forces from Sitten. They were supported by about 3,000 volunteers from Bern,[122] Freiburg and Solothurn. The battle started as a meeting engagement, when the town levy from Sitten ran into the Savoyard advance guard and thought it was the enemy's entire army. During bitter fighting that initially was not going well for the Wallisers, reinforcements arrived at a propitious time. According to legend, the men from the church community (*Zehnden*) of Goms, who were under their leader Anthelm Aufdereggen, brought about a turning point. The Bernese got the retreating Wallis units – also with force of arms – to return to the fighting. Then the Savoyards fled in panic and left about 1,000 dead – among them 300 nobles – on the battlefield. Six wagons with armor, weapons and equipment as well as some banners and 120 warhorses became booty for the Wallisers and Swiss.[123] Then in sequence, the Wallisers conquered all of Unterwallis (Lower Valais) as far as St. Maurice and occupied the Great St. Bernard Pass, before a ceasefire was concluded with Savoy in December.

In the meantime, Charles ended the siege of Neuss that had lasted for eleven months without success. On 26 June 1475 he finally withdrew his forces from Neuss. His next objective was the Duchy of Lorraine (*Herzogtum Lothringen*) that was the land bridge between his northern and southern territories. For this endeavor, Duke Charles sought allies. The Burgundian Duke made a request of the Electoral Prince Friedrich I of the Palatine (*Pfalz*) to provide him military assistance against the Duke of Lorraine, but the Electoral Prince refused.

A delay resulted from the alliance between Charles and his brother-in-law, King Edward IV. Their common goal was to finally defeat France. The English ruler wanted to be crowned in Reims as the King of France, a claim that the English had kept alive despite their defeat in the Hundred Years War. A role was contemplated for Duke François of Brittany who was to invade France reinforced by an English expeditionary corps of 2,000 men. The English should – or in any case the Duke of Burgundy wanted them to – land in Normandy like they had done in the Hundred Years War.

But the English-Burgundian cooperation did not have an auspicious start. During June the English brought their forces to their possession in Calais that was encircled by Burgundian territory. They marched through Burgundian lands but that did not occur without pillaging. When King Edward himself joined his army on 6 July, there was no sign of a Burgundian army.[124]

On 14 July 1475, Duke Charles arrived in the English King's headquarters with 50 horsemen. The English were peeved about the late arrival of the Burgundian Duke. Even worse, was that despite English expectations, Charles had brought along no battle-ready army. Instead he presented a campaign plan that seemed logical but which aroused mistrust in the English camp. King Edward wanted to advance together with the Burgundian forces from northern France toward Paris. However, Charles planned a pincer attack: The English in the north and the Burgundian army in the east should force the French mon-

---

[117] Sitten, in French "Sion", is located in Valais/Wallis. The "*Domkapitel*" of a bishopric supported the bishop in the leading and administration of his diocese.

[118] That was the church communities in the Oberwallis (Valais) canton.

[119] A *condottiere* was "(1) a leader of a band of mercenaries common in Europe between the 14th and 16th centuries also; a member of such a band; (2) a mercenary soldier". (https://www.merriam-webster.com/dictionary/condottiere) It is also spelled "Griffi".

[120] Literally translated it is "free archers", but they were in no way all archers, but also some men armed with hand-cannons and pole-arms or pikes.

[121] He was the Duchess's brother-in-law. In older descriptions he was sometimes cited as the "Bishop of Geneva", which could not be correct because he was never ordained as a bishop.

[122] The core of the volunteers was comprised of levies from the countryside of (Bernese) Saanenland and the Simmental (Simmen Valley).

[123] See Furrer, Sigismund, *Geschichte von Wallis, Band 1* (Sion Calpini & Albertazzi, 1850), p. 219.

[124] See Turnbull, Stephen, *The Book of the Medieval Knight* (London: Crown, 1985), p. 177.

arch into a two-front war that would have forced Louis XI to split his forces. At the same time Charles could conquer Lorraine. But the French devastated the estates from which the English had hoped to obtain supplies, and fighting began near St. Quentin. At the same time King Louis XI made diplomatic offers to Edward IV and in early August 1475 a change of mood occurred. The fact that he had furloughed a portion of his combat-weary troops while holding the other half ready for a campaign against Lorraine fostered the English's tendency to quit the planned campaign against France. Charles appealed to his brother-in-law but could not prevent a decision to his disadvantage. On 29 August 1475, the English and French Kings met on the bridge of Picquigny[125] and concluded a treaty. It established a seven-year ceasefire and the English forces withdrew immediately from French soil. This arrangement was sweetened for Edward by a one-time payment of 75,000 crowns *(écus à la couronne)* and an annual pension of 50,000 crowns from the French King's purse; in return Edward promised to have his daughter Elizabeth of York wed the French royal heir as soon as the couple had reached a suitable age.[126] That Edward was still calling himself the "King of France" did not especially bother the realistic Louis XI. Charles the Bold did not want to attack France by himself, particularly since his war chest was no longer full. The 13 September 1475 Treaty of Soleuvre with the French King brought Duke Charles some room to maneuver. He turned to a different objective, even though his army was no longer in the best shape.

Charles' campaign against Lorraine ran relatively simply nonetheless. The artillery he drew together for the campaign was impressive: six bombards, six smaller bombards, six mortars, ten "*courteaux*",[127] 17 large "*Serpentines*" and 48 smaller ones.[128] The Burgundian forces advanced in two attack columns: a strong assault force under the command of the Neapolitan *Condottiere* Cola di Monforte, Count of Campobasso,[129] attacked from the north, followed by more forces under the command of the Duke himself. That force quickly conquered the north of Lorraine, while another army and the leadership of his half-brother Antoine occupied the south. The army under the Duke's personal command moved up the Moselle River and then turned north in the direction of Nancy.[130] With his typical recklessness and cruelty, Charles the Bold struck fear and terror into the hearts of Lorraine's populace. A Frankish nobleman, Wilwolt von Schaumberg, serving in his army reported that during the storming of the town of Charmes, Schaumberg's tent had stood under a tree from which 37 soldiers from the Lorraine garrison had been hung afterward. In order to enter the tent, one had to duck under the feet of the dead, but then a tree limb broke and the corpses lay halfway on the tent. But one didn't dare ask the Duke permission to set up the tent elsewhere.[131]

In October and November 1475 the Duke's army completely[132] occupied [133] Lorraine. In Nancy, Charles proclaimed himself the new Duke of Lorraine and bestowed on himself the insignia of Lorraine duchy. The presence of representatives from the European princely courts, and even a papal legate, at the ceremony gave the usurpation of the title of the Duke of Lorraine an undeserved legitimation. Charles promised to be a just prince. He made Nancy the new capital of Burgundy.[134] He rewarded his army commander, Campobasso, with lands including domain over Commercy (Bas-Château), Pierrefort and Einville-au-Jard.[135] To Charles, Lorraine was of course far more important than the area bordering the Swiss Confederation. For his enemies on the Upper Rhine, Lorraine was a more urgent matter than the Jura and Waadt (Fr.: Vaud) too. From Lorraine, Charles could move into Alsace. That was naturally evident to the Alsatians as well. So when Duke René of Lorraine sent a request for assistance to the Lower Union, the Allies immediately agreed. Strassburg sent 500 footsoldiers and 300 horsemen, Basel and Freiburg sent contingents, Colmar, Schlettstadt and Thann did the same. The Bishop of Strassburg sent 800 soldiers; Baron (*Freiherr*) Wilhelm von Rappoltstein sent 50 horsemen and 60 footsoldiers. When the Allies caught sight of how many forces Charles was having march into Lorraine, they quickly sent 800 men and four cannon to strengthen Nancy's garrison and moved back into Alsace. Consultations with the presence of French emissaries took place in Colmar, where it was decided to continue the war against Duke Charles and that forces from the Lower Union should move toward Lorraine in three march columns. Then news arrived from Épinal that Burgundian forces were besieging the town. It was defended by troops from Lor-

---

125 It was a wooden bridge built over the Somme especially for this purpose.
126 In January 1476 the relations were further improved through the conclusion of a trade treaty.
127 That was a light cannon.
128 See Vaughan, p. 222.
129 See Walsh, Richard J., *Charles the Bold and Italy, Politics and Personal* (Liverpool: Liverpool University Press, 2005), p. 344.
130 See Bennet, Matthew and Hooper, Nicholas, *The Cambridge Illustrated Atlas of Warfare: The Middle Ages, 768–1487* (Cambridge: Synopsis, 1996), p. 149.

131 See Vaughan, *Charles the Bold*, p. 356.
132 Only Lorraine's Saarburg (Fr.: Sarrebourg) didn't fall into the Burgundians' hands. The town's population was split into a pro-Burgundian party to which the ruling class belonged, and an anti-Burgundian party. However, in February 1476 the Saarburg council accepted a garrison from Strassburg.
133 Nancy, protected from him by Meinrad Schütz, fell on 26 November 1476 after about a one-month siege; on 30 November Charles ceremoniously entered the city.
134 See Ehm-Schnocks, Petra, p. 199.
135 Campobasso had temporarily been in the service of the Angevines in Naples and John of Calabria-Lorraine had transferred Commercy to him. The displaced Duke René of Lorraine was his nephew.

Grandson Castle
Photo: Archipat from Wikipedia /License CC BY-SA 3.0

raine, French contingents[136] and 700 Alsatians under the leadership of Captain Wilhelm Herter. In Épinal, Jean de Vaudémont[137] held overall command of the Allies. While part of the town's populace enthusiastically supported the bravely fighting Alsatians, the other Lorrainers did not show as much enthusiasm. The town had to be handed over (on 19 October), but Herter was allowed to depart in peace with this troops.

On 17 November 1475, Duke Charles agreed to a betrothal of his daughter Maria to the Kaiser's son Maximilian. This settled the Burgundian Duke's conflict with the Empire. The Emperor then put pressure on the Imperial Cities to no longer support the Swiss in their fight against the Duke of Burgundy. And it only got worse for the Swiss: King Louis had concluded a nine-year peace with Charles in the 13 September 1475 Treaty of Soleuvre. Indeed, he involved his alliance partners, though he also informed the Swiss that he would not support them if they did not cease their hostile activities against Burgundy. Additionally, he made an agreement with Charles that the latter could reoccupy the regions on the Rhine and was permitted to go to war in the Swiss Confederation if the Swiss should oppose him.

With this, Louis flagrantly violated his treaty with the Swiss Confederation. He had now pulled the strings in a manner that he finally achieved what he had always been striving for: he had successfully forced the Swiss Confederation into a war with his archenemy Burgundy. France itself, thanks to the peace treaty with Charles, could keep out of the war and watch how the two adversaries tore each other to shreds. King Louis was able to very accurately analyze the personalities of his opponents and anticipate their next moves. That was definitely due to the advice of Philippe de Commynes who knew Charles very well. Supposedly it was he who first foresaw that the Burgundian Duke would become irreversibly entangled in the conflict with the Swiss and their allies. Furthermore, the Treaty of Soleuvre gave the French crown a bonus. A price Duke Charles had to pay for this treaty - whose implications he certainly did not understand – was that he had to deliver the Connetable of France,[138] Louis I de Luxembourg, Comte de St. Pol, over to the French King. Guy de Brimeu, Sire de Humbercourt, handed over the prisoner to a French delegation at the border. The Connetable was a commensurate intriguer. When things on French soil had become too dangerous for him because of his very treasonous activities, he had fled to Burgundy.[139] When

---

136 In older descriptions there is talk of Gascons, see Kirk, John Forster, *History of Charles the Bold, Duke of Burgundy*, Vol. III (London: 1868), p. 184.

137 He was an illegitimate son of Count Antoine de Vaudémont and was therefore named "Batard de Vaudémont".

138 The Grand Constable of France.

139 On 16 December 1475 he was sentenced to death for "lèse-majéste" and three days later executed before a large public gathering. The Comte de St. Pol was the father of Jean de Luxembourg who had been in the Burgundian service in high positions at

Site of the Burgundian camp at Giez
Photo: Thomas Vaucher

news about the Grand Constable's handover to the French crown arrived at French units in Lorraine, who were so reliant on Duke René's support, they withdrew immediately. But the Duke of Lorraine was not only one who felt betrayed and sold out.

The Swiss suddenly were without the support they thought they had for certain from powerful France – and now they had not only the formidable Charles the Bold, who was now the designated father-in-law of the son and heir of the Holy Roman Emperor, as an enemy. Then their allies' small battlefield successes became more marginal. In November the Bishop of Basel's troops captured the castle of Maîche, on 25 November, the 191 representatives of the inhabitants of the Freibergen (Fr.: Franche-Montagne) region swore allegiance to the Bishop of Basel.[140]

In the beginning of February 1476, in the valley of Rotenberg (Fr.: Rougemont), a select unit of cavalrymen under the command of Friedrich Kappler (who was still the commander in Héricourt) attacked Charles' English mercenaries, killed thirty of them and took another thirty prisoner, including their commander, and seized sixty horses.

The Alsatians prepared for the Duke of Burgundy's impending attack. In Strassburg, buildings - 620 houses and five monasteries - surrounding the city wall were torn down.[141]

The Basel Council recruited a few hundred men with hand-cannons in Nuremberg, Ulm, Überlingen and Rottweil. They had the Master Jos cast a new large cannon ("*Hauptbüchse*") called the "*Widder*" ("Ram") and had Master Konrad Tugy produce large quantities of gunpowder. Veltin von Neuenstein, a veteran of many wars who had fought for Basel as a mercenary since 1473, was hired for life.[142] Along with these very sensible precautions, there was also one very curious one: They had heard of a miracle worker in Nuremberg named "Heinrich der Visierer" (Henry the Visor-Maker) who pretended to have found a substance to make walls secure from being stormed and to make it impossible to penetrate a city. He was immediately summoned to Basel.

---

court and in military functions. Fate's irony is that not even two years later, Humbercourt was captured by the citizens of Ghent, accused of high treason, and finally beheaded on 3 April 1477. See Kleiman, Irit Ruth, *Philippe de Commynes, Memory, Betrayal, Text* (Toronto: University of Toronto Press, 2013), p. 153.

140 This vow occurred in the Kallenberg (Fr.: Chauvilliers) castle whose occupants had already changed many times during this conflict.

141 See Smith, Robert Douglas and DeVries, Kelly, *The Artillery of the Dukes of Burgundy, 1363–1477*, Woodbridge: ABC CLIO, 2005, p. 188.

142 He was the offspring of a Basel knightly family and was considered – not unjustly – as being very happy to fight. In May 1473, Veltin von Neuenstein entered the employ of the City of Basel and in September of that year obligated himself by a contract to perform service with three horses and two men-at-arms.

Burgundian infantry Photo: Susan Sümer

DESCRIPTION OF A DEPLOYMENT OF A SWISS CONTINGENT

(Departure of the Forces from St. Gallen before the Battle of Grandson)

"The Elector-Abbot Ulrich sent out a missive from [the town of] Wil to his congregations and ordered them to send two men to the Residence in St. Gallen who should listen to his directives regarding the military preparations to be undertaken. They heard that the Abbott was considering raising 155 men, and two pipers, two wagon drivers and five horses, that, therefore, fourteen men each from the towns of Wil and Tablat were still due, and two each from Gossau, Waldkirch, Straubenzell and Rorschach, etc., and that the troop must assemble for departure in the next days (the date was probably set as 24 February).

Meanwhile in the monastery itself there was busy activity. Rope makers, smiths, wagon wrights, saddlers and shoemakers were being gathered, a cart wright from Magdenau was hired, the heavy "*Reiswagen*"[143] was serviced and loaded with all the necessities. It was loaded with 170 arrows (crossbow bolts?), two barrels, two large field cauldrons with ladles and hooks, eight bowls, a quarter ("*Viertel*"[144]) of salt and more than two "*Malter*"[145] of oats that had already been cooked with salt and lard. The Abbot selected as captain Baron Peter von Hewen zu Hohentrüns (a citizen of Wil since 1472) who had joined his service almost exactly one year before (on 22 February 1475). The church's flag was again entrusted to a respected Wil burgher, Konrad Grossmann. The Abbott gave Grossmann 20 guilders and Peter von Hewen 50 guilders for the way. Thus, the people departed the Prince's lands on a tough daylong march in order to reach the Confederation's army that was then starting on its way via Bern to Neuenburg (Neuchâtel). Their neighbors from the City of St. Gallen, 131 men under Captain Ulrich Farnbüler who had the confidence of the citizenry at home and in the field, had hurried ahead of them".

(From: *Historischer Verein in St. Gallen (Hg): Neujahrsblatt* (St. Gallen 1861) [The Historical Association in St. Gallen, New Year's Edition]

---

143 A "*Reiswagen*" appears to be a wagon pulled by some draught animals.

144 A "*Viertel*" appears to refer to one quarter of a "*Nösel*", a former German unit of volume whose precise size varied according to location and material measured; generally in the range of 100 to 200 liters. In general, the *Nösel* (also spelled *Össel*) was a measure of liquid volume equal to half a *Kanne* ("jar", "jug", "bottle", "can"). Its subdivisions were the *Halbnösel* ("Half-Nösel") and the *Viertelnösel* ("Quarter-Nösel"). Source: Wikipedia.

145 A "*Malter*" is a German term for a former unit of volume whose precise size varied according to location and material measured, generally in the range of 100 to 200 liters. (Source en.wiktionary.org).

THE BATTLE OF GRANDSON

For his part, Charles the Bold lost no time. On 11 January 1476 he left Nancy with strong troop contingents and arrived in Besançon on the 22nd.[146] Then he marched through the Jura toward Waadt (Vaud), in the winter crossed the snow-covered 1,008 meter (3,307 foot) Jounge Pass, and very soon re-conquered the recently lost Savoyard region. Those few Bernese garrison troops who had been left there retreated into the Grandson castle and left the conquered areas of Waadt to the enemy mostly without a fight. They only continued to hold Yverdon. At the same time the Swiss were sent an alarm and requested to have a relief army rush to help the men in Grandson. On 13 January, Jacques de Romont[147] made a surprise attack on Yverdon. Supposedly he had maintained contact with the town's populace through the *Discalceati* (*Barfüßerorden* or Order of Barefooted Monks And Nuns) as intermediaries. The nighttime attack, called the "Yverdon Night of Murder" ("*Iverduner Mordnacht*") resulted in Bernese losses. However, some of them were able to save themselves in the castle. While reconnoitering, Brandolf von Stein, the Bernese garrison's commander, fell into the hands of the Burgundians (allegedly some Swiss in the Burgundian service captured him), and he was held under close arrest.[148]

On 19 February 1476, Charles arrived at Grandson with his army that numbered about 15,000 men. A first attack was repulsed, yet on 21 February the Burgundians forced their way into the small town and the Bernese garrison – 500 men under Captain Hans Wyler – had to withdraw into the castle. The castle's siege lasted a week. The Burgundian artillery had basically shot the castle to pieces, destroyed the Bernese gunpowder supply and killed their artillery captain (*Büchsenmeister*) along with others. The Burgundian nobleman Jean de Rondchamps using insincere promises convinced the Swiss to surrender. They even paid him 100 guilders as thanks for his negotiations with the Duke, before they opened the gate to the Burgundians on Ash Wednesday, 28 February.[149] It is unclear whether or not the Duke's decision to give no mercy to the Bernese garrison was possibly based on a request by the Vaudoises who had suffered much under the Bernese. In any case, the next day, in a four-hour execution, every last one of the 412 men were drowned in the lake or hung from the trees – drowning and hanging were considered dishonorable methods of execution.[150]

Execution of the Bernese garrison of Grandson from the chronicle of Johannes Stumpf

On 29 February Duke Charles was able to secure the Vaumarcus castle northeast of Grandson whose owner, Count Jean de Neuchâtel-Vaumarcus, had opened the gates to him. The castle controlled the road along Lake Neuchâtel (*Neuenburgersee/Lac de Neuchâtel*). A Burgundian garrison under George de Rosimbos, made up of troops from the ducal household, was placed in the castle. A Burgundian detachment in a field fortification, called the "Burgundian Redoubt" ("*Redoute des Bourguignons*"), secured a path that was somewhat further from the lake. The main body of the Burgundian army camped about two kilometers (1¼ miles) northwest of Grandson at the village of Giez.[151]

In the meantime, about 18,000 to 20,000 Swiss and Allies gathered at Neuenburg (Fr.: Neuchâtel) without knowing that the garrison in Grandson had already been executed. On 1 March, the Allied army camped at Bevaix on Lake Neuchâtel. The army mostly consisted of troops from the Swiss Confederation. The Confederation's allies and dependent territories (Fribourg, Biel, Solothurn, Baden, Schaffhausen, Appenzell and the City and the Abbey of St. Gallen) provided 2,800 men and the Lower Union more than 3,000 men.

---

146 See Zellweger, Johann Caspar, *Geschichte des Appenzellischen Volkes* (Trogen: Meyer und Zuberbühler, 1834), p. 98.

147 He was a high noble closely related to the Savoyard ducal family and also one of the most talented commanders in the Burgundian army.

148 See Stierlin, Rudolf Emanuel, *Die Burgundischen Kriege* (Bern: Huber und Comp. Körder und Fehr, 1840), p. 27.

149 Philipp von Hachberg-Sausenberg, who served in the Duke's army, supposedly promised during negotiations that the Burgundians would treat the Grandson garrison honorably. See Rodt, Emanuel von, *Die Kriege Karls des Kühnen, Herzogs von Burgund und seiner Erben, Band 2*), p. 52.

150 A legend states that the Burgundian Duke spared the lives of two Bernese, Hansli Kranz from Latterbach and Peter Happach, because they helped execute their own comrades. See Rochholz, Ernst Ludwig (ed.): *Eidgenössische Liederchronik* (Bern: C. Fischer, 1842), p. 162.

151 A small pond established by the Burgundians for watering horses still exists today.

Battlefield terrain of the Battle of Grandson (near Concise), the Burgundians' vantage
Photo: Thomas Vaucher

The Swiss Confederation members provided:
- Zurich: 1,701 men (commanded by Heinrich Göldli[152] and Felix Schwarzmurer),
- Bern: 7,343 men (commanded by Petermann von Wabern),
- Luzern: 1,861 men (commanded by Heinrich Haßfurter),
- Uri: 458 men,
- Schwyz: 1,181 men (commanded by Rudolf Reding),
- Unterwalden: 455 men,
- Glarus[153]: 780 men (commanded by Hans Tschudi),
- Zug: 434 men.

The allies and dependent territories stood up the following contingents:
- Fribourg: 828 men,
- Biel: 213 men,
- Solothurn: 928 men,[154]
- St. Gallen (City): 131 men,
- St. Gallen (Abbey): 151 men,
- Baden: 286 men,
- Schaffhausen: 106 men[155],
- Appenzell: 200 men.

The units of the Lower Union were organized as follows:
- Basel: 1,200 men,[156]
- Strassburg: 259 men,
- Colmar: 35 men,
- Schlettstadt: 26 men,
- Rottweil: 100 men,
- the "Forest Towns" ("*Waldstädte*"), Sundgau and the Black Forest Domains (*Herrschaften des Schwarzwalds*): 1,500 men.[157]

---

152 He, along with many others, was dubbed a knight after the battle.

153 Including Thurgau.

154 They were commanded by Conrad Vogt.

155 They were led by the Old Mayor (*Altbürgermeister*) Ulrich Trüllerei.

156 The large Basel contingent supposedly included men from the Basel City and the Princely Bishopric.

157 See Heath, p. 40. "Waldstätte" was the name used since the 19th century for the region referred to as the 'original Switzerland' (German "Urschweiz"), relating to the locations of forested mountainous country. The term "Waldstatt" first appears in a document from 1289. In this context Waldstätte refers to Uri, Schwyz and Unterwalden in Central Switzerland. Source: Wikipedia

Battle of Grandson from Diebold Schilling's Berner und Spiezer Chronik (ca. 1483). Wikipedia

Additionally, there were 200 horsemen provided by Duke Sigismund and smaller contingents from southern Germany, such as 50 lancers from Augsburg (under Count Ludwig von Oettingen) and 60 footsoldiers from Nördlingen (under Captain Gabriel Ehringer).[158] There must have also been some men from Graubünden (Fr.: Grisons) in the Allied army.

During the night of 1 to 2 March 1476, the Swiss attacked the Vaumarcus Castle, and the Burgundian Duke learned about it.

On the morning of 2 March, the Swiss departed from their camp in two columns, and on the same morning Charles set his army in motion. That was a major operational mistake by the Duke because the positions at Grandson were advantageous to Duke Charles. Both parties were aware of the opponent's army, yet for both sides the collision of the advance guards of their armies at Concise was a surprise because neither the Swiss nor Charles had considered conducting a thorough reconnaissance.

The Battle of Grandson happened almost by chance when the Burgundians' advance guard, which wanted to move into an encampment, ran into a Swiss lead unit. The Swiss and their allies had marched down from the mountains with Lake Neuchâtel on their left. Thus, the advance guard was far ahead of the main body and the rearguard. The Swiss had passed by the Vaumarcus castle.

They had a "lost unit" of gunners, archers and crossbowmen, consisting of 100 men from each Bern, Schwyz and the City of St. Galllen, whose advance guard had been sent ahead.[159] Whether these people were supposed to be foraging or had been sent out ahead for security, they ran into the Burgundians. Against strict orders from their captains who wanted to wait for the return of other army units, the Swiss advance guard marched further forward. Fighting developed between Duke Charles' long bowmen and Swiss "archers", who according to stories were hand gunners from Schwyz. They held the upper hand in the fighting. In the meantime, the Swiss main body had advanced closer. Duke Charles had arrayed his forces in battle order; his plan was to fire upon the enemy forces with artillery and afterwards to defeat them with his cavalry.

The Swiss deployed in square formations with standard bearers and halberdiers in the middle and pikemen around them. The hand gunners formed a thin flanker screen in the front and on the flanks. The Swiss placed a few artillery pieces on their right flank. The Burgundian cavalry, with the Ducal Guard in the second wave, then attacked in a wedge formation. The skirmishers were scattered and fled literally to the feet of their own pikemen and sought protection under the forest of the long pikes that the ducal cavalry could not penetrate. The fighting was the heaviest on the Burgundians' left flank where a Burgundian cavalry unit under Louis de Chalon attempted to outflank the Swiss main body. In the process fierce hand-to-hand fighting ensued during which Louis de Chalon was killed.[160] According to legendary tradition, the 27-year old high noble tried to seize the Schwyz banner but in the attempt fell from his horse and was killed with a halberd.[161] More Burgundian cavalry attacks followed. The terrain was unfavorable for the Burgundian attacks in that they had to charge uphill. Charles seems to have made the incorrect assumption that the Swiss advance guard was the entire Swiss army. He wanted to pull back his center that consisted of foot soldiers in order to draw in the solidly standing Swiss main body (it was only the advance guard) and thus carry out stronger attacks from the flanks. He gave the units in the center of his battle formation an order to pull back a little. Companies of bowmen and handgunners were to be repositioned on the flanks. His cavalry units, which had still not been engaged in the fighting, were massed on the left flank in order to strike the decisive blow. Just as the Burgundians began to carry out the complex maneuvers, the Swiss main body and rearguard appeared on the battlefield and immediately went into battle formations. All three Swiss large formations then advanced slowly. Then the Burgundian foot soldiers thought the tactical rearward movement in the center was the sign of a defeat and they began a wild flight to leave the battlefield. Duke Charles could not stop his footsoldiers from fleeing and he also could not hold up the Swiss advance by renewed attacks by his cavalry. So he and his cavalry left the battlefield.

---

158 See Würdinger, Josef, *Kriegsgeschichte von Bayern, Franken, Pfalz und Schwaben, Erster Band* (Munich: Literarisch-Artistische Anst. der Cotta'schen Buchhandlung, 1868), p. 130.

159 See Embleton, Gerry and Howe, John, *Söldnerleben im Mittelalter* (Stuttgart: Paul Pietsch Verlag, 1996) (Published in English as *The Medieval Soldier: 15th Century Campaign Life Recreated in Colour Photographs*, London: Windrow & Greene, 1994), p. 20.

160 Another prominent fatality on the Burgundian side was Pietro dei Corradi di Lignana. Command of his Ordonnance Company went over to his son Guglielmo dei Corradi di Lignana. Also killed were Quentin de Baume and Jean de Lalaing.

161 In another incredible story passed down, it was Hans von der Grub from Bern who killed Louis de Chalon. Von der Grub, who belonged to the *"Berner Rossbanner"* (Bernese Horse Banner), sprung forward and grabbed Louis de Chalon, and stabbed him to death with a *"Spießlein"* (a short lance). See Rodt, Emanuel von, *Die Kriege Karls des Kühnen...*, p. 79.

In Diebold Schilling's powerful language it appeared as: *"da warend die langen Spies zuringumb die Panern gestalt, nach Ordnunge der Houptlühte und Vennern, die man jnen gar mannlichen in die Nasen sties, damit sy sich bald widerkarten, und von dannen raw ten, doch blieb todt ligen, der vorgenant Herr von Tschettegion, der ward von einem Burger von Bern umbbracht, hies Hans von der Grub, und ander mit ihm"*.

"The long pikes were arrayed around the banners, according to the orders of the captains and standard bearers ("Vennern"), which one thrust in their noses in a most manly way, so that they turned away and ran, indeed left lying dead, the forenamed Lord von Tschettegion, who was killed by a citizen of Bern, named Hans von der Grub, and another with him".

That decided the battle, Duke Charles was forced to take flight and leave behind his baggage train and artillery. But the Swiss and their allies lacked the cavalry needed to pursue the defeated Burgundian army. There were only Habsburg vassals and Swabian troops, together with a few hundred men under Count Oswald von Thierstein. Along with them were a few horsemen from the "Bernese Horse Banner" ("*Berner Rossbanner*"). To chase after the still not essentially weakened Burgundian cavalry would have been unwise. So they the victors contented themselves with executing Grandson's Burgundian garrison that had surrendered. They simply threw the Burgundians they found in the castle from the walls, except for a Burgundian nobleman, whose name is passed down as Jehan de la Tour. Before his planned execution, prudent Allied captains saved his life so they could exchange him for Bradolf von Stein. Then they got busy taking the booty home. In the Swiss camp before that, Hermann von Eptingen, who had led Duke Sigismund of Tyrol's mounted auxiliaries in the battle, dubbed many men from Bern, Zürich, Strassburg and Basel as knights. Peter Rot, the Basel Captain made a joke[162] when sending a letter to the Council of Basel by sealing it using the signet stamp belonging to Antoine de Bourgogne, the Duke's half-brother, who had fallen into his hands. The Swiss had bypassed Vaumarcus Castle during their movement, and in the night the Burgundian garrison escaped leaving behind their horses and baggage.

Charles the Bold did not lose many men (estimates range from 300 to about 1,000), but the booty taken by the Swiss and their allies that day was enormous.[163] They captured 1,500 wagons, 300 barrels of gunpowder and thousands of packhorses. A richly decorated sword belonging to the Duke was among the booty; decorated with seven diamonds, seven rubies and fifteen large pearls, as recorded by Schilling in his "*Bernese Chronicle*" ("*Berner Chronik*").[164] The silver-plated bathtub was also among the booty.[165] Also the most splendid of Duke Charles' magnificent hats changed owners. That treasure was made of red satin and decorated with pearls and jewels. A Swiss soldier put on the hat, and then took it off with the words that his helmet fit him better – figuratively - he was right. The Swiss also captured two of Charles' silk tents, decorated with jewels and gold embroidery. An unexpected prize was the numerous -supposedly 2,000 - "*filles de joie*" (French for "prostitutes).[166]

Along with money and the valuable objects, the Swiss captured 419 cannon that Charles would painfully lack in his later campaigns.[167]

The Swiss pillage the Burgundian camp
from Diebold Schilling's Chronicle

---

162 Veltin von Neuenstein had actually been granted a field command, but he was with Duke Sigismund of Tyrol on a diplomatic mission.

163 In April 1476 Glarus, in the name of the *Tagsatzung*, complained to Graubünden, which did not yet belong to the communities that joined the Confederation but out of its closeness with the Confederation had provided troops at their request, that they should hand over spoils and add them to the booty, which should be fairly divided.
Ironically at this time there was a small but bloody war between the House of God Alliance ("*Gotteshausbund*", one of the three alliances) and the Tyroleans in Lower Engadine (*Unterengadin*) (the so-called "Hennenkrieg", see page 98 below).

164 See Remy, Andreas, Descriptions of Battles in Fifteenth Century Urban Chronicles, in Curry, Anne and Bell, Adrian R., *Journal of Medieval Military History, Vol. IX* (Woodbridge: Boydell and Brewer, 2011), pp. 118–131, especially p. 128.

165 See Davies, Norman, *Verschwundene Reiche, Die Geschichte des vergessenen Europa* (Darmstadt: Konrad Theiss, 2013), p. 159. Published in English as *Vanished Kingdoms: The History of Half-Forgotten Europe* (London: Penguin, 2012).

166 That was far more than the embarrassingly exactly set number of thirty "camp girls" per the Burgundian Duke's army structure allowed per Ordonnance company.

167 According to one source, the booty included 400 large cannon ("*Hauptbüchsen*"), 800 hand-cannon ("*Hakenbüchsen*" – early harquebuses), 27 main banners, 550 flags and 400 tents. See Ebel, J.G., *Anleitung auf die nützlichste und genussvollste Art die Schweitz zu bereisen, 3. Teil* (Zurich: Orell, Gessner, Füssli & Compagnie, 1810), p. 147.

THE BATTLE OF MURTEN/MORAT

Above all, the Duke of Burgundy's pride had indeed been injured. He was said to have neither eaten nor drunk for two or three days. He was laid low and appeared primarily to be psychologically stricken.[168] His "*Valet de Chambre*", Jean le Tourneur, reported the Duke having bouts of rage. Charles made a vow that he would either die in battle or defeat the Swiss. He then categorically ruled out negotiations. The Swiss were also in no way satisfied with what had been achieved. On 3 March the Héricourt garrison – reinforced by some Basel and a couple Strassburg troops – under the command of Friedrich Kappler carried out an attack in Franche-Comté. At Montbozon they ran up against Burgundian forces under the hated Stephan von Hagenbach. According to a legend, he had dressed sixty women in men's clothing in order to have his forces appear larger than they really were. Even though Kappler's men, who were in marching order, were surprised by the Burgundians they were able to drive off the enemies and cost them 26 dead. On Kappler's side there were only one wounded and one dead.[169] Also a small garrison of men from Zurich stationed in Fribourg under the command of Hans Waldmann carried out forays into Burgundian territory. In April and May troops from the Lower Union under Basel's leadership attacked into the Burgundian region multiple times.

On 8 April, the levy from the County of Greyerz (Fr.: Gruyères)[170] destroyed the Châtelard castle whose lord, Pierre de Gingins, had conducted guerrilla warfare from there against the Wallisers (Valaisoises).

In March, the Wallisers, for their part, attacked the town of Villeneuve and destroyed it; on 10 April they appeared before the Castle of Chillon. The small garrison had been hastily reinforced by 40 crossbowmen, and the Wallisers were not able to capture the castle.[171] However, on 8 June 1476, 800 Bernese, mostly men from the Obersimmental, commanded by Nikolaus Zurkinden, stormed the town of La Tour-de-Peilz on Lake Geneva, captured the castle, which was courageously defended by Pierre de Gingins and his men, and carried out a horrible massacre of the inhabitants.[172] Lombard mercenaries, coming from the Simplon Pass through the Nanz Valley, moved in order to join up with the Burgundian army. The Wallisers almost entirely wiped out the several hundred-man Lombard unit.

The news of the Duke's defeat at Grandson took a few days until it reached Speyer. At that time Wilwolt von Schaumburg was stopped there. He had been in the Duke of Burgundy's service since 1473. After the siege of Neuss and the campaign against Lorraine, he and some of his German friends in the Duke of Burgundy's army had requested leave so they could purchase new clothes and equipment. When the news of the catastrophe at Grandson reached him, he decided not to return to his master.

After the Battle of Grandson, the Swiss *Tagsatzung* (Assembly) issued a new set of wartime regulations on 18 March 1476. It was intended to strengthen the forces' cooperation in the field, to better concentrate all their forces to attain the main goal of a battle, namely the complete destruction of the enemy's military. It was strictly forbidden to take prisoners, especially in order to receive ransoms. Experience had shown that taking prisoners significantly distracted the combatants and the bulk of the enemy was therefore able to escape.

Charles now focused his attention more directly on the Swiss Confederation, than the general military situation demanded, since in Lorraine, which he considered the heart of his empire, there were after all rebellions against the Burgundians. In April 1476, the town of Vaudémont successfully rebelled against its Burgundian garrison. According to passed down information, the Burgundian Duke's remaining allied princes advised him against a new military operation against the Swiss - it would bring no glory to deal with these peasants. Allegedly it was already clear to the princely courts in Italy that a decisive struggle between Burgundy and the Swiss Confederation could certainly end favorably for the latter, and then the Swiss (not to mention the French King) would be a threat to the northern Italian princes.

Immediately after the defeat at Grandson, Duke Charles set about assembling a new army. He sent Hugues de Chalon, Seigneur de Château-Guyon,[173] to northern Italy where he was to recruit mercenaries. However, the Duke of Milan put the brakes on these recruiting attempts.[174] Charles completed rebuilding the artillery: In the County of Burgundy each house's father had to hand over half of the iron dinnerware and horse tack to the prince's foundries where people were working day and night to produce new cannon. But that was not enough to make up for the

---

168 See Dubois, Henri, *Charles le Téméraire* (Fayard: Fayard le Grand Livre du Mois, 2004), p. 403.

169 His name is actually known, it was Caspar der Schneider, a kitchen servant of the Duke of Tyrol. See, Vulpinus, *Ritter Friedrich Kappler*, p. 56.

170 In the past, the counts of Greyerz/Greyères had often been the allies of the Counts of Savoy. According to legend, Count Rudolf IV of Greyerz, who was supposed to conquer Wallis on behalf of Count Amadeus VII of Savoy, was defeated on 23 December 1388 in Visp by the residents of the town of Visp and the Oberwalliser rural inhabitants in the so-called "Battle on the Blue Stone" ("*Schlacht am Blauen Stein*").

171 See Rodt, Emanuel von, *Die Kriege Karls des Kühnen*, p. 145.

172 See Fatio, Guillaume, *Au tour de lac Léman* (Geneva: Institut Polygraphique, 1902) Reprinted by Rother Verlag, Oberhaching, 1981), pp. 126–128.

173 He was the younger brother of Louis de Chalon who had died at Grandson. He survived the Burgundian Wars, married Louise de Savoy, the daughter of the Duke of Savoy in 1479, and died in 1490.

174 See Walsh, *Charles the Bold and Italy*, pp. 30–31.

In the Holy Roman Empire, the German term *Hochstift* (plural: *Hochstifte* or *Hochstifter*) referred to the territory ruled by a bishop as a prince, as opposed to his diocese, generally much larger and over which he exercised only spiritual authority. Source: Joachim Whaley, Germany and the Holy Roman Empire, Oxford University Press, 2012, volume 2, Glossary of German terms and other terms.

Gruyère Castle
Photo: Thomas Vaucher

loss of all the cannon at Grandson. Although some new cannon were manufactured, the artillery of the newly raised Burgundian army consisted mainly of older pieces. Charles assembled an army of around 22,000 men. He divided it into four divisions, with the first commanded by Julio d´Acquaviva, the Duke of Atri. Federico de Aragon, the Prince of Taranto, commanded the second division.[175] The third was under Jean de Luxembourg, the Count of Marle and Soissons; and the fourth under Jacques de Romont. A reserve unit was created, whose command Duke Charles later passed to his half-brother Antoine. Within Charles' army there was a series of clashes between the Italian mercenaries and the other nationalities. The Italians especially did not get along with the Englishmen. In the first week of May, the English joined with men from Flanders, Wallonia and Picardy to plunder the Italians' encampment. A major bloody conflict could only be prevented with great effort. However, about thirty dead were left behind.

The Burgundian Duke had decided on having a decisive battle against Bern, however, he did not know which route of advance he should take. On 9 May, in the presence of the Duchess of Savoy, Duke Charles held a large review of the army and demonstrated confidence. In his camp, the word was they were to go against Murten. That was discovered by a spy from Bern who immediately returned to Bern to report his observations.[176]

The Bernese were not unaware of what happening on the Burgundian side. They evacuated the small towns of the Waadt (Vaud) and pulled back into Savoyard Murten that had been in their hands since October 1475 and had strong fortifications. They increased the garrison to

---

175 He was the son of King Ferrante I of Naples and for a long time he was under discussion as the possible husband for Charles' heiress Maria. His father had sent him to the court of Charles the Bold where he was supposed to serve as a counterweight to the Neopolitan exiles, especially Campobasso.

176 See Walter, Bastian, "*Urban Espionage and Counterespionage during the Burgundian Wars (1468-1477)*", in: Curry, Anne and Bell, Adrian R., *Journal of Medieval Military History*, Vol. IX (Woodbridge: Boydell and Brewer, 2011), pp. 132–145, specifically p. 139.

Above the roofs of Murten
Photo: Michael Gauger

2,000 men – 1,500 Bernese and 500 Freiburgers. To that were added some cannon from those taken at Grandson that would now be used against their former owners. In the face of this threatening disaster and in order to prevent a catastrophe like at Grandson, they were looking for a competent commander for the town of Murten. They found one in the former mayor of Bern, Adrian von Bubenberg, who had been banned from the Council of Bern on 10 July 1475 because he had always spoken out for an alliance with Charles. Bubenberg has spent part of his upbringing as a nobleman at the Burgundian court and had gotten to personally know Charles while there. According to legend, they were even friends. However, Bubenberg's loyalty and patriotism were never questioned. On 8 April 1476, Adrian von Bubenberg took over command in Murten. He had the houses outside the town walls torn down, and small boats made ready that could guarantee the town would get emergency supplies from across the lake. Furthermore, he had sufficient provisions stockpiled to hold out during a siege. His strict regimen was to make it clear to the garrison that the town would never surrender.

Bern armed itself to fight Charles. In addition, the Council of Bern requested help from the other Confederation members, but it got negative replies because Murten belonged to Savoy and not to Bern. The other Confederation members wanted to have nothing to do with Bern's expansionist policies, but only if Bern itself were to be attacked, would they intervene. Also, Louis XI, whom Bern reminded of his treaty obligations, would not think of rushing to their aid, and so Bern stood (almost) completely alone against the might of the Burgundian Duke, or so it appeared. The tone of the letter that the Council of Bern sent to Ulm, Rottweil, Nördlingen and other Swabian cities was telling. It spoke of the need to defend "the common German nation" ("...*die gemayn tütsche Nacion*"). "The enemy of all of us" ("*Unser aller vyend*") is the "Burgundian Duke, whose disposition is completely hot" ("*Burgunderhertzog, dessen Gemut in gantzer Hitz*").[177]

Swiss Soldiers Cross the Alps
from the Lucerne Chronicle

On 9 June, Charles' army arrived before Savoyard Murten and began the siege. However, the Murten garrison still had access via the lake so, above all, news could be transmitted from and to the town. The Burgundian Duke had his headquarters – in splendid tents, as was his custom – set up on a hill. He received guests there, like the English traveler Anthony Woodville, Earl Rivers, who was just returning from a journey to Italy. Rivers was (like Charles) related by marriage to King Edward IV of England and when Rivers wanted to join the Duke's service, he even offered him a command position in the army. However, Earl Rivers rejected it when he learned how near the Swiss had already advanced. He bade Duke Charles goodbye and departed. That contributed to Woodville's reputation among his English critics as a coward.

On the hills above Murten, where he expected the Bernese relief army to attack, Charles had a hedge strengthened in a makeshift manner and built a palisade style line of defenses with it, the so-called "*Grünhag*" ('Green Hedge').[178] On the north end of the *Grünhag* he positioned a 200 meter-wide line of artillery that could flank the defensive works. The left flank of the artillery was protected by a deep defile, the so-called "*Burggraben*" ('Castle Ditch' or 'Castle Moat'). The Burgundian cavalry was to assemble on the south end of the *Grünhag*. Charles' plan was to let the enemy's army run into the *Grünhag*, fire upon them with the artillery from the flank, and then execute the decisive cavalry attack from the other flank.[179] He had an army of about 22,000 men to carrying out the plan. But of them, many were not combatants. He had more than 5,700 archers/handgunners, 5,100 footsoldiers,[180] 2,100 heavy cavalrymen and a few hundred light cavalrymen.[181] Then he made a mistake that would have serious consequences: the Bernese relief force that was certain to arrive, so in order to fend off the arrival as early as possible, Charles attempted to capture the bridges at Gümmenen and Laupen. Those bridges were essential to crossing the Saane River if one wanted to go from Bern to Murten. On 12 and 13 June there were bloody engagements on both bridges, but which the Bernese decided in their own favor. Now the Burgundians had indeed attacked Bern's territory and Bern's renewed calls for assistance to the other Confederation members were finally heard. The Confederation took up arms and marched to Murten. Because the members in eastern Switzerland had a much longer distance to go, contingents arrived on the scene intermittently – the Bernese first, then those from Solothurn, those from the Waldstätten and so forth. There were very varied contingents among them, e.g., some men of the 'Land Flag of Hauenstein ("*Hauensteiner Landfahnen*") from the Black Forest and the around 200-man strong levy of the Count of Greyerz, Johannes III von Montsalvens. Above all, one had to wait for the arrival of the large Zurich force under Hans Waldmann. He with just the core of his force – 200 Zurichers and a few hundred men from Freiburg – had marched from Freiburg to Bern where they joined with the main

---

178 The *Grünhag* was between 800 and 1,000 meters (875 and 1,100 yards) long and its construction begun on 17 June 1476 was an impressive accomplishment for the Burgundian army.

179 See Geiger, Benjamin, "*Die Burgunderkriege, Die Schlachten von Grandson und Murten 1476*", in *Pallasch Zeitschrift für Militärgeschichte*, No. 43 (Salzburg: Österreichischer Milizverlag, 2012), p.19.

180 Among the footsoldiers, two contingents should be specifically mentioned: about 350 men from Flanders, Holland and Geldern, and 100 Swiss mercenaries in the Duke's army.

181 In the fight for Murten, Charles the Bold employed a total of twelve *Ordonnance* Companies (according to one source it was 14 *Ordonnance* Companies) of them six were from Italy and three from Savoy.

---

177 Quoted at the time by Ochsenbein, Gottlieb Friedrich, *Die Urkunden der Belagerung und Schlacht von Murten* (Freiburg: Bielmann, 1876), p. 92ff.

Murten with parts of the city Defenses
Photo: Michael Gauger

body from Zurich[182]. The main body had rushed to Bern in a forced march, arriving on 21 June, and then the combined force hurried in the direction of Murten.

In the meantime, a portion of Murten's town wall had succumbed to Burgundian bombarding and collapsed. On 18 June the Burgundians made the fiercest assaults on the town, but Bubenberg and his men repelled six assaults in a row until the nighttime. On the next morning the Burgundians attempted two more assaults that were also repulsed. But now the town was at its end. Bubenberg knew he could not hold the town much longer and sent a messenger to Bern with a request for assistance.

The Swiss assembled at Ulmiz, but not all the contingents had arrived. Among others the strong contingent from Zurich was missing and it was decided to wait a little for them. The non-Swiss portion of the army was considerable: The Imperial City of Strassburg sent 550 horsemen and 300 dismounted hand-gunners, along with twelve field pieces. The Habsburg Steward provided 800 horsemen; Duke René of Lorraine deployed a small corps of 300 horsemen at his own expense.[183] Rottweil sent 50 fighters commanded by Boly der Rüd. The total from the Bishops of Basel and Strassburg was considerably larger, amounting to 1,000 men under Hermann von Eptingen's command. Basel sent even more men: 1,500 footsoldiers and 100 horsemen[184] under the command of Peter Rot. Among the Swiss, some smaller contingents were integrated into the Bernese forces, such as the 100 men from Neuchâtel under the Sire de Cleron or the 200 men from Biel under Adam Göuffi.

---

182 There were 2,000 men under Heinrich Göldli and Frischhans von Breiten-Landenberg.

183 The Duke of Lorraine only had departed Strassburg on Wednesday, 19 June, and had ridden almost without interruption.

184 The horsemen were led by Veltin von Neuenstein.

Light artillery piece, 2nd half of the 15th century
Photo: Anja Hiebinger

The Burgundians also prepared for the coming battle. After they learned of the Swiss army being camped at Ulmiz (about six kilometers east of Murten), the Burgundian army was placed in readiness several times in vain starting on 18 June. The repetitive drawing up in battle formation, for the last time in the pouring rain on 21 June demoralized the troops. That was the day that Duke Charles rode out with a reconnaissance troop to personally observe the Allies' camp. The Burgundians came to a forest from which they received heavy fire from the enemy's hand-gunners, and they turned around.[185] The Duke came to the conclusion that they were still not ready to attack. He was unable to change his belief, as expressed at a war council held the evening of 21 June, where he again reinforced his decision not to have the whole army to form up the next day. On the next morning, Charles did not take seriously scouts' reports that the Allies were moving forward. He also had to change the army's command structure on short notice because Federico of Aragon departed the Burgundian camp – on the express orders of his father, the King of Naples.[186]

The Confederation waited up until Saturday, 22 June, when the forces from Zurich, Austria and Lorraine also arrived and the Swiss and their allies' army had grown to 24,000 men, before they decided to attack. It was preceded by an early morning raid by a large group of allied horsemen led by Wilhelm Herter, Friedrich von Fleckenstein and Veltin von Neuenstein.[187] They scouted out the terrain and reconnoitered the Burgundian positions.

---

185 See Clayton, Anthony, *Warfare in Woods and Forests* (Bloomington and Indianapolis: Indiana University Press, 2012), p. 19.

186 See Calmette, Joseph, *Die großen Herzöge von Burgund* (Munich: Diederichs, 1996), pp. 333–334.

187 According to one source, the forces were supposed to consist of 1,000 footsoldiers (under the Strassburg captain Friedrich von Fleckenstein and Veltin von Neuenstein) as well as 600 horsemen under Wilhelm Herter. See Elgger, Carl von, *Kriegswesen und Kriegskunst der schweizerischen Eidgenossen im XIV., XV. und XVI. Jahrhundert* (Luzern: Militärisches Verlagsbureau, 1873), p. 335.

Andrian von Bubenberg's memorial
Photo: Thomas Vaucher

Artillery scars from the siege of Murten
Photo: Michael Gauger

The commander-in-chief – if there actually was one on the Allied side – could have been Wilhelm Herter von Hertneck from Württemberg.[188] After the army had been divided into an advance guard, main formations and a rearguard and more than 100 men had been dubbed knights, the Swiss army finally attacked around noontime. The advance guard was commanded by Hans von Hallwyl, and the main body by Hans Waldmann from Zurich. According to tradition, the levies from Entlebuch and Thun were with the advance guard. Horsemen under Duke René of Lorraine[189] secured the flanks. The Count of Greyerz and the Count of Thierstein commanded smaller mounted units.[190] On the Burgundian side, the *Grünhag* was only occupied by about 2,000 men and a few deployed outposts because Charles no longer expected an attack by the Swiss that day. Therefore, the greatest part of his army found itself unprepared in its encampment. If it was actually the case that on this of all days, Duke Charles began to hand out the pay to his troops, as some of his contemporaries claim, his army would absolutely not be ready for battle.

If one believes the stories that have been passed down, just as the Swiss army moved out of the woods the rain stopped and the first rays of sunshine broke through the clouds. The first attack on the *Grünhag* was repulsed by the Burgundians, but then a contingent from Schwyz under Dietrich in der Halden was able to cross the steep *Burggraben* defile north of the *Grünhag* and attack the

---

188 The only concrete indication of this is a reference in the diary of the Basel Chaplain Knebel: "*capitaneus totius exercitus confoederatorum(qui) ordinavit bellum contra Burgundum*".

189 It certainly belongs to the realm of legend that the Duke of Lorraine went into battle like a simple Swiss soldier on foot with a halberd. See Daguet, Alexandre, *Geschichte der schweizerischen Eidgenossenschaft von den ältesten Zeiten bis 1866* (Aarau: H. R. Sauerländer, 1867), p. 193.

190 See Pfister, Johann Christian von, *Geschichte von Schwaben, Neu untersucht und dargestellt, 2. Buch, 2. Abteilung* (Stuttgart: Daniel Class, 1827), p. 237. See also Rütz, Dieter, "Die Reiterei der Eidgenossen", in *Die Zinnfigur*, Ausgabe 4, 2017, p. 107.

Burgundian positions from the side. Then the Swiss broke through the Burgundians' defenses and rolled up their positions. The greatest part of the Burgundian army (including Charles himself) was still busy getting armored as the battle's outcome was already decided. Smaller groups of Burgundian fighters arriving in succession were wiped out. The Milanese emissary Panigarola, who experienced the battle directly in the vicinity of the Duke of Burgundy, was amazed that the Duke had acted as if he were paralyzed. Finally, it was too late to influence the course of the battle; the Duke could only withdraw in the direction of Lausanne with his close entourage.

The Murten garrison under Bubenberg also made a sortie. And the Swiss advance guard, 5,000 men under Lucerne's Kaspar von Hertenstein, was able to join in the fighting. The Swiss poured out like a wave over the Burgundian camp and killed anyone within reach of their weapons. And again, the Burgundian troops sought their salvation in flight. But the Swiss rearguard and main body had blocked the escape route. The Burgundian army's Italian division under Troylo de Muro da Rossano was driven into Lake Morat. Those who attempted to save themselves by swimming ran into two small boats from the Murten garrison and they were mercilessly killed. The Savoyards under Jacques de Romont had better luck: their camp was located at Muntelier somewhat northeast of Murten on the shore of Lake Morat. They fought their way free and were able to depart to the northeast.

Various Swiss contingents arrived on site of the battle too late to take part in the fighting, such as 200 from Schaffhausen under Eberhard von Fulach or the 600 from Appenzell under Ulrich Thanner.

In the Strassburger Konrad Pfettisheim's "Rhymed Chronicle" ("*Reimchronik*"), he wrote:

> "*Wol sübczehentusent vnd ouch me*
> *Die wordent do her slagen,*
> *Gar vil ertrunckent in dem se,*
> *Sich huob ein fyntlich iagen.*"[191]

The Burgundians lost 8,000 men and at least as many non-combatants. Among the fallen were also Jean de Luxembourg[192] and Gianfrancesco, a son of Troylo da Rossano.[193] George de Rosimbos was killed, as well as Nolin de Bournonville, the commander of a large unit of footsoldiers. The Swiss and Allies lost between 2,000 and 3,000 men.[194] As always in this period the information about battle losses varied. Panigarola, after all an eyewitness to the events, estimated the number of Allied dead at 3,000.[195] Duke Charles, who loved splendor and was obsessed with power, was devastatingly defeated by the Swiss and their allies. Again, the spoils were enormous.[196]

A cannon that the Swiss had captured caused a particular citizen of Bern serious difficulties. The cannon bore a coat of arms that the Swiss Confederation thought they recognized as belonging to Margrave Rudolf IV of Hachberg-Sausenberg. For a part of his extensive land holdings, the Margrave was a Burgundian vassal and in the past he had served Duke Charles in various functions (as governor of Luxemburg in 1467 among other duties), but he had 'citizen rights' ("*Burgrecht*") in Bern and Solothurn. Starting in 1473, he had withdrawn from the Burgundian court; but his son Philipp served in Charles's army. Philipp's role in the capitulation of the Grandson Castle's Bernese garrison put his father in a precarious situation. He had been summoned to Bern where he had to lodge in the "*Lambachs Hause*" ("Lambach's House") – the best inn in the city.[197] Luckily for Margrave Rudolf, who was temporarily forced to live in Bern, the Strassburgers, who had a similar coat of arms, laid claim to the cannon.

The many captured suits of armor were exhibited as trophies in the Swiss communities – often in churches. Since the Swiss were for the most part footsoldiers, they had little use for the Burgundian mounted knights' armor and it did not always fit them (due to differing physiques).[198]

---

191 Quoted from Tobler, Gustav, *Conrad Pfettisheims Gedicht über die Burgunderkriege* (Bern: K. J. Wyss Erben, 1917), p. 23. Roughly translated from medieval German as "Indeed seventeen thousand and even more, were killed there, very many drowned in the lake, and were hunted down."

192 According to a passed down account, he offered a ransom of 25,000 Ducats if he would be spared, but that is doubtful.

193 The Duke of Somerset was definitively not among the dead as sometimes claimed in older accounts. Henry Beaufort, 3rd Duke of Somerset, was executed in 1464. His brother, Edmund Beaufort, who claimed the title, died in the Battle of Tewkesbury on 6 May 1471.

194 The number of 400 Swiss dead that is sometimes found in sources seems to be too low, even if the Alsatians, Lorrainers, etc. are not counted in the total. See Boué, Gilles, "*Grandson and Morat*" in Sandler, Stanley, *Ground warfare, An International Encyclopedia*, Vol. 1 (Santa Barbara etc.: ABC CLIO, 2003,) p. 333.

195 See Heath, p. 86.

196 That 2,000 "*Lagermädchen*" ('camp women') also fell into the victors's hands is often claimed but can hardly be verified. See Pfister, Christoph, *Die alten Eidgenossen: Die Entstehung der Schwyzer Eidgenossenschaft im Lichte der Geschichtskritik und die Rolle Berns* (Norderstedt: Paul Haupt, 2013), p. 243.

197 See Rodt, Emanuel von, *Die Kriege Karls des Kühnen*, pp. 104–105. Later the Count was released to his Rötteln Castle, however under heavy Bernese guard. The strong presence of Bernese in the Rötteln domain caused Basel discontentment.

198 See Oakeshott, Ewart, *European Weapons and Armour: From the Renaissance to the Industrial Revolution* (Woodbridge: Boydell and Brewer, 1980), p. 79.

THE BATTLE OF NANCY

After the victory at Murten, a portion of the Swiss forces and an Alsatian contingent went pillaging through the Waadtland (Fr.: Vaud) as far as Lausanne. They fought against Savoyards and the troops of the Bishop of Geneva. Friedrich Kappler and his squadron of horsemen as well as 400 men from Basel under Veltin von Neuenburg were part of this contingent led by Wilhelm Herter. French King Louis XI intervened and initially brokered a ceasefire and later a treaty between the Swiss and the Savoyards. On 27 August 1476, the Basel captain Meinrad Schütz entered the area of Besançon with 1,500 men. Even though he had received the Basel Council's authorization, it was actually more of a thieving spree.

On 16 August, Charles the Bold issued a decree that threatened each of his vassals with the confiscation of all of their property if they did not personally appear for military duty or pay a special tax of one sixth of their annual income. After the Battle of Murten, the Milanese Duke, Galeazzo Maria Sforza, terminated this alliance with Charles and signed a treaty of friendship with French King Louis XI. Charles, who had first gone to Salis and then to La Rivière after the battle, was in no way as depressed as he was after Grandson. According to the observations of the Milanese emissary Panigarola he was very confident. The Duke, who tended toward self-glorification, saw the catastrophe at Murten as a kind of divine test, which a hero, as he saw himself, would pass. That was a sign of his increasing loss of reality. Anyway, he had his forces occupy the Jura mountain passes to be prepared for attacks by the Swiss. However, he neglected to send adequate forces to the Lorraine theater of war in a timely manner, in order to strengthen the garrison at Nancy. The ducal governors quickly mastered the problem of groups of deserters moving around Burgundian territory by summarily hanging them.

When, after a meeting with Duke Charles, Duchess Jolanthe of Savoy (she was the French King's sister) instead of going to Burgundian St. Claude as promised, returned to Geneva, Charles felt justified in kidnapping his alliance partner and her children. He tasked Olivier de la Marche, the commander of his personal guard, to do this. Although he was plagued by bad premonitions, he loyally carried out the order on the night of 26-27 June, but the young Duke Filiberto[199] evaded him. Lodovico Taglianti d´Ivrea was responsible for that. He was the commander of one of the Burgundian army's Ordonnance Companies, and as a subject of the Dukes of Savoy, his conscience bothered him. He brought the young Duke Filiberto and the younger brother Carlo to safety with the help of other Savoyards.[200] In the meantime, the Duchess, whom La Marche abducted on his horse, was carried over the Jura Mountains to Saint-Claude and then further to Rouves Castle near Dijon. That brought about an abrupt end to the alliance with Savoy. In Geneva there was a bloody uprising against the Burgundian forces. King Louis XI was later able to free his sister. Seigneur de Chaumont with 200 lancers retrieved Jolanthe from Rouvres and escorted her to Langres. And he took over as the Protector of Savoy, with which Charles accomplished exactly the opposite of what he had wanted to achieve. He apparently blamed the fiasco on Guillaume de Rochefort who left the Burgundian court. Charles gave him eight days to return, and then Rochefort was declared an outlaw.[201]

Then Charles finally desisted from his plans of revenge against the Swiss because in the north Duke René of Lorraine threatened the land bridge between his northern and southern domains. Charles' governor in Lorraine, Jean de Rubempré, Seigneur de Bièvre, was in dire straits. The supply line, which ran through the Bishopric of Metz, whose Bishop Georg von Baden supported Charles, did not help.[202] In Lorraine a group of noblemen under the leadership of Jean de Vaudémont[203] had joined together on their own initiative to fight against the Burgundian occupiers. Duke René left Strassburg to help them, accompanied by a 600-man Strassburg reserve unit with two large cannon and ten "Serpentines".[204] He successfully besieged Lunéville with them. The Burgundians could not hold the town and the commander, Giovanni di Monforte,[205] handed it over. Then the Duke of Lorraine aimed at Nancy. He received reinforcements from Basel, which sent ten horsemen and 160 footsoldiers.[206] The commander of Nancy's Burgundian garrison did everything within his power to hold the city. A unit of English bowmen commanded by Henry Colpin was also part of his command. Colpin was a brave man who had worked his way up from

---

199 Born on 7 August 1465 in Chambéry; since 1472 he was the successor to his late father Duke Amadeus IX as the Duke of Savoy. But his mother, Jolanthe, exercised the regency. Filiberto died young, on 22 September 1482, in Lyon.

200 See Walsh, *Charles the Bold and Italy*, pp. 350–351. Lodovico Taglianti d´Ivrea came from one of the famous Condottieri families, and some of his relatives had already served in the Duke of Burgundy's army. He rose to high state office under Savoyard Duke Carlo III, whom he had saved as a boy from the Duke of Burgundy's clutches.

201 He later entered French service and in 1483 became the Chancellor of France.

202 The Bishop had concluded an alliance treaty with Duke Charles on 29 September 1473.

203 With him were Count Simon Wecker IV von Zweibrücken and Count Philipp von Leiningen.

204 A contingent from Basel under Veltin von Neuenstein was with them.

205 Giovanni di Monforte was the son of the Count of Campobasso. He handed over Lunéville with the approval of his superior, Jean de Rupembré.

206 They were under the command of Veltin von Neuenstein. On 11 October Basel sent 200 men as reinforcements.

simple conditions. When a cannonball killed him, it was the end of discipline of his men, who had belonged to the English garrison of Guines before their employment in the Burgundian army. The end of September 1476, these 300 English mercenaries mutinied in the city (certainly mostly because of not getting paid) and departed. On 6 or 7 October Rupembré, who could not get any help overcoming the acute lack of provisions, capitulated.[207] In exchange for being allowed to leave peacefully he handed over the city and Duke René entered.

A few weeks earlier, the Duke of Burgundy had already decided to protect "his" new capital, Nancy, with all his means and at any price. On 25 September he left his field encampment in La Riviere and marched via Besançon, Vesoul, Joinville, Bulgnéville and Neufchâteau toward Toul. When he arrived in Toul on 11 October, just a couple days after Nancy had fallen, he had only the choices of withdrawing or continuing with the attempt to recapture the city that had been lost in the meantime. He decided on the latter course without considering the inadequacy of his forces. To gain Nancy by force of arms was at this time a risky game.

Charles definitely wanted to take back Nancy and on 22 October he arrived with his forces before the city. His army – compared with the standard of earlier days – was small. He mobilized what he could. In mid-November, 123 heavy cavalry, five 100-man companies of mounted archers and 2,700 footsoldiers arrived from the northern parts of Flanders, Artois, Hainaut and other lands. An additional ordonnance company arrived the beginning of December. But enemy activity between Thionville and Nancy made it very difficult for the Burgundian Duke to provide supplies to his forces in the northern regions. He urged his governor in Luxembourg, Claude de Neuchâtel, Sire du Fay, almost pleadingly to do something about it.[208] The last known letter from Duke Charles' quill was written on 31 December 1476. It included a desperate request to Claude de Neuchâtel to send supplies to the camp at Nancy. The winter was unusually harsh, which made military operations more difficult for both sides.[209]

Duke René of Lorraine had among his forces a large contingent of Alsatian footsoldiers, mostly men from the City and Bishopric of Strassburg. They were undisciplined and demoralized. Even though the Steward Wilhelm von Rappoltstein (who had succeeded Oswald von Thierstein in this function) had tried to raise a contingent of Alsatian noblemen cavalry, no cavalry accompanied the footsoldiers. The proud nobles refused to join the fighting until their owed salaries had been paid. A contingent of 400 Alsatian footsoldiers mistakenly saw a Burgundian camp as their allies, marched up to it, and found themselves unprepared for an attack by the Burgundians. The Alsatians were easily dispersed. René II of Lorraine left 2,000 men behind in Nancy and went to the Swiss Confederation to ask for help. But the Assembly (*Tagsatzung*) hesitated. Schwyz, Glarus and Unterwalden refused, using the rationale that it was too cold for a campaign (which was not completely incorrect). Bern and Fribourg said they feared a Burgundian attack from the west. Lucerne, Zurich and Solothurn promised to have their contingents move out, but only if the other Swiss went as well. Finally, King Louis promised the practically bankrupt René 40,000 guilders with which to recruit mercenaries in the Swiss cantons assuming the permission of the *Tagsatzung*. In any case, Basel and Strassburg guaranteed the sum. For that time the formidable offer of an excessively exorbitant monthly pay of four guilders (later four and one half guilders), quickly brought in a crowd of 8,000 to 10,000 men. The mercenaries' assembly point was Basel. In the autumn of 1476, Wilhelm Herter, who had been the commander-in-chief at the Battle of Murten, also went into Duke René's service. Other allies recruited mercenaries in Switzerland, for example, Strassburg hired 300. Basel sent out 500 men under the command of Bernhard Schilling, not as mercenaries for the Duke of Lorraine, but as a levy of the Lower Union.[210] That unit went up the Rhine by ship. The Alsatian contingents joined them at Colmar. Then they went via St. Dié and Lunéville.

The chroniclers reported about a gruesome episode regarding one of the Duke of Lorraine's messengers, Siffredo dei Baschi, who the Burgundians caught trying to enter the city. In one of Duke Charles' war councils there was disagreement about what should happen to Siffredo dei Baschi (who was described as either Italian or Provençal). Duke Charles had him hanged within view of Nancy, which Nancy's inhabitants answered by hanging a Burgundian prisoner.[211]

The beginning of January Duke René returned to Nancy with his new army where the situation had become precarious due to the harsh winter and the siege. But the situation in the Burgundian camp was also tense, with the morale seeming to have reached a low point. Four hundred men died due to the cold. A soldier – a knight according to legend– suggested they should actually shoot the Duke of Burgundy into the city with a large cannon. He was hanged for this impertinence.[212]

On 5 January 1477 the battle began before Nancy. Shortly before it began the actual overall command was passed from René of Lorraine to Wilhelm Herter and

---

207 Rupembré had treated the city's population justly and had acted with a certain understanding with regard to its interests.

208 See Vaughan, p. 423.

209 See Crowe, Eyre Evans, *The History of France*, Vol. 1 (London: Longman, Brown, Longmans and Roberts, 1830), p. 159.

210 See Wackernagel, p. 100.

211 The number of 120 hanged Burgundians cited by Müller seems very high. See Müller, Johannes von, *Die Geschichten Schweizerischer Eidgenossenschaft* (Reutlingen: Mäcken'schen Buchhandlung, 1825), p. 441.

212 See Smith, Robert Douglas and DeVries, Kelly, *The Artillery of the Dukes of Burgundy, 1363–1477*, p. 199.

The Battle of Nancy
Old etching

Oswald von Thierstein (for the cavalry).²¹³ The reason was that the Allied war council did not consider the militarily inexperienced Duke to be up to the task. The young Duke – conspicuously dressed in a cloak interwoven with gold over his armor – sat at the head of his cavalry, in which the Counts of Bitsch, Leiningen and Salm were located, and the indefatigable Jean de Vaudémont was there too. The 26-year old Antoine de Ville, Sire de Domjulien, carried Lorraine's main banner.

The Allies' commander led about 19,000 men in the fighting against the Burgundian army that was hopelessly outnumbered. They were located somewhat south of Nancy at Siechenhause La Madrlaine near the village of Jarville. As Charles the Bold was trying to mount his black warhorse, allegedly his golden helmet crest fell off. He saw that as a bad omen. ²¹⁴

---
213 A smaller squadron of horsemen was commanded by Wilhelm von Rappoltstein.
214 See Sporschil, Johann, *Die Schweizer-Chronik, Von der Stiftung des Rütli-Bundes bis zum ewigen Frieden mit Frankreich* (Leipzig: Kayser, 1840), p. 604.

Duke Charles had positioned his artillery in front of his battle line. The cannon were not of the same quality as those he had lost at Grandson. Obviously, the Duke's plan was to only have them fire one salvo since there was no time to reload.

The Burgundian army's left wing consisted of men under the leadership of the knight Josse de Lalaing; the center (predominantly footsoldiers) was commanded by Duke Charles and his half-brother Antoine, who was called the "*Le grand bâtard*" ("the Grand Bastard") because of his impressive body size.

The Burgundian army's right wing consisted above all of Lombards and was commanded by the *Condottiere* Giacomo Galeotto. Cola di Monforte, the Count of Campobasso, also had his place in the battle ranks here. The Count (who had for some time no longer received his pay from the Burgundian Duke) had tried before to join the

French forces located at Toul. Because there was a cease-fire in effect between the French crown and Burgundy, he was rejected.[215]

Duke René at the head of his troops

Now Campobasso defected with 800 horsemen to the enemy. [216] But the enemy was distrustful (nobody trusted Campobasso) and kept their distance.[217] Campobasso and his men occupied a bridge over which the Burgundians' withdrawal route would run. Now the Allies advanced in two columns from the south, the center struck out far to the left, the advance guard to the right. During a snow flurry the Allies were able to occupy a hill on the Burgundian army's right flank. Allegedly they were guided by two Swiss who had served in the Burgundian army and now in return for a promise of amnesty by their countrymen, they showed them a favorable route to attack. From there, the center with about 8,000 footsoldiers and 1,000 horsemen under the leadership of Wilhelm Herter stormed the entrenched Burgundians after the Horn of Uri had sounded their enemy's doom. The Burgundian Duke's horsemen had still been able to do well against Lorraine's cavalry, but the Allied footsoldiers decided the battle. The Burgundian artillery could not effectively stop the assault. Its cannon were badly positioned, and those that engaged in the fighting fired too high. Supposedly the Burgundian artillery killed only one man from the Allied army. Charles sent a large contingent of longbowmen from his left to his endangered right flank, but it was too late.

Old representation of the Count of Campobasso

The Allied advance guard then struck the Burgundian left flank. The Burgundian cavalry under Giacomo Galeotto was pushed back over the ford of Tomblaine. The battle then devolved into many small melees in which the Burgundians lost at least 6,000 men. Among those killed were also Jean de Rupembré, the Burgundian governor of Lorraine, Ferry de Cusance and others. Many Burgundians drowned in the Meurthe River because the way over the bridge was blocked by the deserters under Campobasso[218]. A group fled up to the gates of the city of Metz where they were taken for thieves or beggars because of their ragged clothing and were not let into the city. Only after one of the Burgundian soldiers was recognized, was the group granted admittance. Others did not have so much luck – the peasants in the area fell upon them and killed them.

The spoils the Allies took were naturally not so great as a few months earlier at Grandson or Murten, but they were still considerable. Burgundian flags arrived in the Solothurn arsenal, Charles's chalice picked up off the ground by the ordnance master Heinrich Strübin[219] went to Liestal whose soldiers had reinforced the Basel corps.

---

215 See Vaughan, p. 425.

216 Campobasso had not taken part in the campaign against the Swiss. After the capture of Nancy, he was granted leave in which he made a pilgrimage to Santiago de Compostela. Because he had to traverse French territory to do so, many suspected that he treasonously made contact with the French crown.
On 2 January he departed with some horsemen, and somewhat later his sons Angelo and Giovanni followed with more horsemen. See Shaw, Christine, *Barons and Castellans, The Military Nobility of Renaissance Italy* (Leiden and Boston: Brill, 2015), p. 110.

217 According to Diebold Schilling it was a question of honor for the Swiss: "*Und wesend die eidgenossen als erlich und loblich harkomen, das sie kein meyneiden man nie hetten wellen unnder inen liden*." Roughly translated as "And while the Swiss came honorably and praiseworthy, that they never would have accepted anybody who swore a false oath among their ranks."

218 Campobasso marched with the remnants of his *Ordonnance* Company to northern Italy where in the early autumn he joined with Venetian forces in Friaul who were preparing for a campaign against the Turks. He died in July 1478 in Padua.

219 He was the proprietor of the "Zur Sonne" inn in Liestal.

Some high-ranking Burgundian army leaders, among them Olivier de la Marche, were captured. Philipp von Hachberg-Sausenberg remained captive until September 1477. He paid 150,000 guilders, the highest ransom of all the Nancy prisoners.

During the rout, Charles suffered two lance stab wounds in the thigh and the lower abdomen and then died from a halberd blow that split his skull. His ransacked and disfigured body was found the night of 7 January. Allegedly the Roman youth Battista Colonna, the Duke's noble page, had seen him fall and could identify the location. Colonna, the Duke's Portuguese personal physician Lopo da Guarda, Charles' half-brother Antoine and Baudouin, as well as Olivier de la Marche were able to identify the Duke based on a missing tooth, an ingrown toenail, and the unusually long fingernails.[220] The victorious Duke René had Duke Charles initially buried in his St. George Court Church in Nancy. Decades later the coffin was transferred to the Church of Our Lady in Bruges. Charles the Bold found his final resting place there.

A baker from Strassburg supposedly had killed the Duke of Burgundy; however, other participants in the battle also made this claim.[221] In the meantime, men from Strassburg took parts of the Duke's clothing home, as well as eight Burgundian army flags that were hung up in the Strassburg Cathedral. They remained hung there until 1531 when the magistrate ordered their removal.

As was already the custom, the chroniclers offered other versions of the Duke of Burgundy's death. Claude de Bauzemont, Steward of St. Dié and a knight from the Duke of Lorraine's retinue supposedly killed the Duke of Burgundy. When the Duke saw that he would be defeated by superior numbers, he allegedly tried to yank his horse around.[222] Bauzemont struck the horse and caused the Burgundian to fall. Charles the Bold identified himself and asked for mercy but the rather hard of hearing de Bauzemont supposedly had not heard.[223]

Charles the Bold's death (old engraving)

Charles the Bold's body is found
(old engraving)

---

220 See Monter, William E., *A Bewitched Duchy, Lorraine and its Dukes 1477–1736* (Geneva, 2007), p. 23.

221 The Duke's wounds indicate they were from a halberd or a similar weapon.

222 See Domke, Helmut, *Flandern – Das burgundische Erbe* (Munchen: Prestel, 1972), p. 22.

223 Eugène Delacroix was inspired by this version of the event for his 1831 painting "La Bataille de Nancy", that hangs in the Musée des Beaux-Arts in Nancy. See Charles, Victoria, *Art of War* (New York, 2010), p. 112.
Also, in Sir Walter Scott's story "Anne of Geierstein", it is Bauzemont who kills the Duke of Burgundy. Oddly enough, the "Lorraine" version of Charles' death shows up only rarely in newer descriptions.

THE AFTERMATH

Charles the Bold died without any male heir. His daughter Maria of Burgundy married the Kaiser's son Maximilian von Habsburg on 21 April 1477, as had been arranged by her father and Emperor Friedrich III. Yet French King Louis XI strove for Burgundian territories. He marched into Dijon and occupied the duchy, and his soldiers laid waste to the border regions in the north. But Maximilian, as the trustee for his wife's inheritance, was able to militarily hold most of the old Burgundian domain including the rich regions of Flanders and the Brabant. In the August 7, 1479 Battle of Guinegate[224] an army consisting primarily of Flemish, Walloon and Picardy troops was able to defend against a French attack.[225] The later Kaiser Maximilian fought with a pike like a simple footsoldier along side the infantry. Previously high-ranking officials for Charles, such as Jacques de Romont and Count Engelbert II of Nassau and Vianden, had command positions in Maximilian's army. After the catastrophe at Nancy, many from that milieu joined the French crown, like Philippe de Crèvecœur who commanded the French army at Guinegate. Philipp von Hachberg-Sausenberg married Maria of Savoy, Duke Filiberto's sister. After the Duchy of Burgundy's return to the rule of the French crown, he became the Marshal of Burgundy.

Wilhelm Herter had already died on 2 March 1477 in Basel. Friedrich Kappler had the most noteworthy career among the commanders on the Allied site: he fought in the service of the Habsburgs against Venice and France, he fought in the 1499 Swiss War (already somewhat aged) and in the 1504 War of Landshut Succession.

Duke Sigismund had regained the "*Pfandlande*" ('Leased Lands'), but acted unwisely and was heavily indebted, i.e., to the Fugger banking house. Emperor Friedrich III took advantage of the foolish policies of his advisors, the Bad Council ("*böse Räte*"),[226] and disempowered this court camarilla, incidentally with the full agreement of the Tyrolean *Landstände* in January 1488. Two years later Maximilian took over the rule of Tyrol and all of Outer Austria ("*Vorderösterreich*")[227] from Arch Duke Sigismund, who died in 1496. The alliance with the Swiss Confederation, the "Eternal Direction" ("*Ewige Richtung*") also belonged to the political legacy. The negotiations about its extension, however, ultimately failed.

The Swiss Confederation, which had been victorious in the Burgundian Wars, entered a short period of internal unrest. The distribution of the enormous spoils from the Burgundian Wars played an important role. After the Battle of Nancy, during the Carnival ("*Fastnacht*") season, the so-called "*Saubannerzug*" ("Sow's Banner March")[228] began. It was made up of soldiers who had taken part in the struggle against Burgundy who tried to forcibly obtain the 'Pillaging Sum' ("*Brandschatzungssumme*") that Geneva had promised. The number of participants in the demonstration was estimated at 1,700 men. The cantonal authorities were definitely in an awkward situation and pacified the demonstration participants with money and wine. With the Treaty of Stans ("*Stanser Verkommnis*") of December 1481 the Swiss Confederation consolidated itself from within. The conflict between the rural and urban cantons had been sparked by, among other causes, the question about admittance of Freiburg and Solothurn to the Confederation. The argument was resolved after tough negotiations following the intervention of the hermit Niklaus von Flüe and the agreement strengthened the Confederation significantly.[229]

---

224 Now called "Enguinegatte".

225 The so-called 'hereditary enmity' ("*Erbfeindschaft*") between France and Germany ultimately grew out of this military conflict.

226 In the historical accounts from earlier centuries it was not proper to criticize a prince's bad decisions. One often just referred to the corrupting influence of advisors. In Duke Sigismund's case it was actually so; his court council drove him to bad decisions in both foreign and fiscal policies.

227 He handed over the government to Maximilian in Innsbruck on 16 March 1490, but he retained an annual pension of only 52,000 Rhenisch guilders, free hunting and dwelling rights throughout the entire country and seven castles.

228 The contemporary chroniclers do not use this expression.

229 See Messner, Florian; Ollesch, Detlef; Seehase, Hagen and Vaucher, Thomas, *Der Engadiner Krieg* (Eltville: RWM Bureau, 2016), p. 57.

Burgundian horseman
Photo courtesy of Daniel Rosenfeld

THE ARMIES AND WEAPONS OF THE BURGUNDIAN WARS

The Burgundian Army

In the medieval Europe standing armies did not exist yet. There were indeed some beginnings in northern Italy and French King Charles VII's military reforms in the 1440s that went in that direction. The armies of the medieval empires in continental Europe were made up of feudal levies that were sometimes strengthened with mercenaries and with militia from the cities. Also, the armies that the Duke of Burgundy took into the field (mostly against France) partially consisted of feudal levies. A vassal with his retinue went into battle with the army for his liege lord. City militias were very important for the Burgundian dukes, especially the militias from Flanders and Wallonia. In addition, there were recruited mercenaries, mostly from northern Italy, England and southern Germany. The combatants from the ducal household formed a core force that was directly obligated to the Duke. All these parts of the army came together only in times of need and in varying combinations. One cannot speak of a standing army. Several points, given the structure of Charles the Bold's forces, could lead someone to come to the incorrect assumption that he had a standing army. The assumption, which would have been revolutionary at that time, rests on several points. The most conspicuous factor is the fact that the ambitious Duke of Burgundy was almost continuously at war. Along with that he had vastly enlarged the military entourage of the ducal court – in 1470 it was almost 2,000 men. Furthermore, he created *ordonnance* companies that remained together longer than just the duration of a campaign. On the other hand, it must be realized that the *ordonnance* companies were not only deployed based on military considerations, but also based on economic factors. The costs for the quartering and upkeep were to be apportioned to the regions. [230] Additionally the warlike Duke's requirements for personnel were so great that he frequently had to fall back on his vassals and on militias from the cities and towns. Actually the Duke of Burgundy preferred to employ the urban militias for garrison duty and to rely on the *ordonnance* companies in the field.[231] For example, for the capture of the Ortenberg Castle in Alsace in November 1470, the Steward Peter von Hagenbach had assembled a very sizeable force of about 5,000 men for the task, and of them 1,200 were mounted troops from the Burgundian *ordonnance* companies, sixty of Hagenbach's mercenaries, and the remainder were feudal levies from the domains and urban militias.[232]

At the time of the Burgundian Wars, armies of knights were a thing of the past, even though many knights did not want to admit that. Strassburg's victory at Hausbergen in 1262 had already shown that the city's footsoldiers had a real chance of victory against the nobility's knightly levies. In the 14th century it was evident that the military dominance of armies of knights had ended. That was clearly shown by the Swiss victories and by the English successes relying on longbowmen in the Hundred Years War. Despite that, the nobility's horsemen, i.e., mounted knights, were still an essential part of the army. If a political leader, like an imperial prince or a steward, in the described period, did not limit himself to the political-strategic management/control or at least the military-operational command, but he actively took part in the actual fighting as a mounted knight (and here the knightly conventions were in contrast to the military requirements), then his actions were in the knightly tradition. And in this context, Charles the Bold immediately comes to mind.

The smallest tactical cavalry unit was the *"lance"* (Fr.: *"lance"*, German: *"Lanze"*), sometimes also called the "glaive" (Fr.: *glaive*; German: *Glefe*)[233]. Both the name and also the structure originated from back at the time of the feudal armies of the High Middle Ages. In the 15th century, the *lance's* nucleus and simultaneously its military leader was the man-at-arms, French *gen d'armes*. He wore armor and carried a lance, corresponding to the cliché of the medieval knight. Despite that, the *lance's* leader by no means had to have ever been knighted. He most frequently carried a hand-and-a-half sword and a short sword or an *espadon* (German: *"Hauschwert"* - the *"Malchus"* or the *"fauchon"*).[234] Other weapons were possibly the mace, the war hammer and the morningstar that had each shown its effectiveness against armored opponents. Although almost all fighters carried some kind of sword as a personal sidearm, the sword was quintessentially the knightly weapon – also the knights' status symbol.

---

230 Although Charles the Bold had a relatively effective tax system and ruled economically robust regions, he often had to borrow money for his campaigns and maintaining his court. He preferred to turn to the Medici banking house in Bruges lead by Tommaso Portinari, to which at the time of his death he still owed 57,000 *"livres"* (pounds). The Burgundians calculated in *"livres tournois"*, and 105 *livres tournois* were worth as much as 100 Rhenish guilders.

231 See Drake, Michael S., *Problematics of Military Power; Government, Discipline and the Subject of Violence* (London: Taylor & Francis 2002), p. 225.

232 In October 1470, Baron (*Freiherr*) Wilhelm von Rappoltstein offered Hagenbach his *"Steinbüchse"* (stone-firing bombard) along with 43 or 44 stone balls and all related equipment, but the Steward had to send him four wagons to transport it.

233 A glaive or *"Glefe"* was a 12th-13th century broad-bladed pole arm in which the edge curves backwards near the point. See below.

234 An *espadon* (or German *"Hauschwert"* (literally a "striking" or "chopping" sword) was a 15th century sword of intermediate size, between the regular and two-handed; much like a hand-and-a-half sword. It had a slightly curved, single-edged blade with fullers on both sides and a double-edged point. It could have simple, 'S'-shaped and curved quillons, a wooden hilt plates and luna-shaped pommel.

Burgundian horsemen
Rear view
Photo courtesy of Daniel Rosenfeld

In addition to the man-at-arms leading the *"lance"*, there was his page, or *valet de guerre*, who usually came from a knightly family – one spoke of being *"ritterbürtig"* (knight-born). He was far more than an officer's orderly in the more modern sense, because at the same time he was learning the art of war. Then there was also a knife-fighter (in France and Burgundy called a *"coutilier"* or *"coustillier"*, or in German a *"Degenkämpfer"*), a squire who was equipped at the *lance* leader's expense. The squire was also armored and armed with a sword or thrusting dagger and usually employed a polearm (like the Ox Tongue [Fr.: *Langue de Boeuf*, German: *Ochsenzunge*], the awl pike [German: *Ahlspiess*] or similar weapon). Additionally, there were three mounted archers, crossbowmen or handgunners and usually three fighters on foot.

It is clear that this formation was not exclusively conceived for cavalry attacking with a leveled lance, but in part was also to be employed as infantry and it had a strong defensive capability. This tactical formation was used broadly, especially in France, Burgundy and Flanders. In the Empire the principle was the same; however, the influence of the Teutonic Knights, i.e., from truly barracks-based units of knights, was still marginally noticeable there. Multiple *"lances"* formed a *"Banne"* (Fr.: *bannière*), whereby its total number cannot be simply derived from the number of lances because a *lance* was often accompanied by different types and numbers of volunteers. The knight-banneret (Fr.: *"banneret"*) served as the banner's commander, who oddly enough did not always have to be a knight. Several "banners" formed a "battle multitude".

In 1445 in France, King Charles VII established the "furnished" or "equipped" "lance" (Fr.: *"lance fournie"*) as consisting of the lance leader – usually a knight, his pages, a *"coutilier"*, two mounted archers and a servant (or common-born man-at-arms). According to this basic model, twenty *ordonnance* companies were formed, each with 100 lances. They formed the foundation of the new professional army in France. There were the Great Ordnance Companies (*"compagnies de grande ordonnance"*) that were favored, enjoyed high esteem and in which the pay was higher. The small ordonnance companies (*"compagnies de petite ordonnance"*) were not as highly regarded but had the same tactical structure. The French King's mounted *ordonnance* companies proved their worth in the Battle of Guinegate on 7 August 1479.

The Duchy of Burgundy copied the French system. On 31 December 1470, Charles the Bold issued an edict on the raising of his own *ordonnance* companies. The nucleus was to be the lance leader – a knight or a squire, like in France. Traditionally there were three social levels that applied under Charles's predecessors and also during the first years of his reign. Initially they were the *"chevaliers bannerets"*, that one could translate as the "banner knights". They came from the social class of wealthy and powerful noble families and had the right to carry their own banner (square or rectangular). Ranked below them were the *"chevaliers bacheliers"*, men from the lower nobility. They were permitted to carry a guidon (with tails). The third group was the *"écuyers"* (squires), who came from the landed nobility or were patricians from the cities and towns. They had to be wealthy enough to pay for their own armor and weapons as well as for that of the men of their *"lance"*. If for any reason that was not possible, the *"écuyers"* often served as *"coutiliers"*. It was also possible to rise through the hierarchy: a *"chevalier bachelier"* could be promoted to a *"chevalier banneret"*. Then the tails of his guidon would be ceremoniously cut off and he then carried a banner. The lance's leader was paid according to his rank. This three-part division ended with the 1471 Ordonnance of Abbeville (*Ordonnance d'Abbeville*). All *lance* leaders were at the same level and all received the same pay. During Charles the Bold's entire reign the vast majority of the *lance* leaders came from the actual Burgundian core regions and from the Artois, but in the last years the number of Italian elements of his cavalry increased sharply.[235] The Duke wanted to raise 1,000 of them, and then he increased the number to 1,200 with the 31 July 1471 Edict of Abbéville. Later he increased the number further. The *lance* leaders were not called *"maître"* like in modern French, but *"condotier"*, clearly showing the Italian influence on the Duke of Burgundy's military thought. In 1473, a Burgundian *ordonnance* company consisted of 100 *lances* each with a *condotier* (lance chief), a page, a *"coutilier"*, three mounted archers and three infantrymen (of those, one was a pikeman, a crossbowman and a handgunner). Additionally, there was a trumpeter for each company.

Moving to the infantry, the Burgundian crossbowmen used crossbows with steel bows that had an enormous range and they could penetrate plate armor if the range and angle of impact were proper. In any case the steel bows tended to break in extremely cold weather. Yet the steel stave helped the crossbow to have a renaissance in regions where they otherwise had been disparaged (e.g., in England). The crossbow bolts were shorter and thicker than longbow arrows. Like arrows, they were "feathered" (fletched), but with small pieces of wood, brass strips or thin boiled leather. By attaching these stabilizers in an angular manner, they were able to cause the bolt to spin. The points of such bolts were four-sided for penetrating armor or "crowned" (similar to jousting lance heads). It was typical for the Burgundian crossbowmen to use large shields that rested on the ground, the so-called "pavis" or "pavoise" that had already gone out of style in other regions. But the Burgundians still used the pavises and frequently painted them with heraldic or allegorical motifs. There was a very efficient crossbow-producing guild in Charles's empire. Toward the end of the 1460s the

---

235 See Michael, Nicholas and Embleton, Gerry, *Armies of Medieval Burgundy, 1364–1477* (London: Osprey, 1983, Men at Arms Series 94), p. 6.

Pavises in the Burgundian colors
Photo: Anja Hiebinger

crossbow producer Luc de Muldre[236] became famous. The crossbowmen usually used a short sword as a secondary weapon, but glaives were also used. A glaive was a pole-arm weapon with a knife-shaped, curved blade that was attached to a shaft by means of a socket or grommet and had a parrying hook on the back of the blade for pulling a rider from his mount.

Burgundy was an innovator with its employing of handgunners ("*couleuvriers*" or "*couleuvriniers*"). There were two basic types of handguns (*couleuvrines à main* – hand culverins) in use. They were actually 'fire pipes", a smoothbore tube of iron, bronze or a copper alloy. It had a touchhole on the end and had a caliber between 13 and 22 millimeters (from ½ to 7/8 inch). The barrel was very short but had very thick walls. At the end of the barrel, a bar was attached that formed a handgrip or a knob. But the barrel could also have a wooden shaft attached. To ignite the gunpowder, the gunner had to hold a glowing wire or a smoldering match to the touchhole and hold the weapon steady with his other hand. Therefore, many

---

236 See Boeheim, Wendelin, *Handbuch der Waffenkunde, Das Waffenwesen in seiner historischen Entwicklung von Beginn des Mittelalters bis zum Ende des 18. Jahrhunderts* (Leipzig: Seemann, 1890), p. 610.

handguns were equipped with a hook under the barrel, as so-called *"couleuvrines à croc"* (culverins with a hook, or German *Hakenbüchsen*),237 with which the weapon could be attached to a parapet. For this type of culverin, the caliber could sometimes be from 26 to 29 millimeters (1" to 1 3/16"). Larger culverins were mounted on supports and served by two men. This category led the way to actual artillery pieces. The precision of these weapons was not very great, aiming hardly possible; one cannot talk about accuracy in this context. The first matchlock muskets were somewhat more accurate and easier to handle. The matchlock weapon was already known in Italy since 1411. A match was hung on an S-shaped fixture, the so-called "serpentine" or "serpentine lock" that allowed the gunner press one end of the serpentine and the other end would touch the match to the igniter pan. Later, the serpentine was moved by spring action when it was released by a trigger. This process, combined with better varieties of gunpowder that burned more evenly, resulted in a more certain ignition and increased the accuracy, somewhat. The Ducal Ordonnance of Bohain-en-Vermandois of 13 November 1472 established that handgunners had to be equipped with a chainmail shirt, a *"gogerin"* (gorget), breastplate and helmet.

The pikemen came mostly from the northern parts of the duchy, especially from Flanders. Their pike shafts were about three-and-a-half to four-and-a-half meters (11 ½ feet to 14 ¾ feet) long and had a shaft from sturdy, vertically-splitting ash. In German the term *"Pike"* (from the French *"piquer"* = to stab) first appeared in the mid-16th century. 238 Because both hands were needed wield the pike, the pikeman wore protective body equipment. On the march, the pike was certainly not shouldered because it would have been risky for his comrades. Additionally, a shouldered pike would have swayed so that it would have bounced up and down. Other than on parades or for similar events, the man grasped the pike a little behind the point and dragged it after himself. In use along with the pike were halberd-like weapons (for example the *voulge* or *guisarme*) that could serve as an engineer's tool when storming a fortification.

The Burgundian *ordonnance* company was commanded by a *"conducteur"*. The "conducteur" designation by itself reveals its Italian influence. In France and in Burgundy before Charles the Bold ruled, the corresponding position was called a *"capitaine"*. Until October 1473, the handover of an *ordonnance* company was conducted with a celebratory ceremony in which the new *"conducteur"* was given a commander's staff, a practice that originated in Italy, more precisely in Venice.239 Until October 1473, an *ordonnance* company consisted of ten detachments each of ten *lances*. Each such detachment was commanded by a *"dizenier"*. 240 He personally led six *lances* in the field, while his deputy, the *"chef de chambre"*, led the other four lances.241 This organization was abandoned with the *"Ordonnance de St. Maximin de Trèves"* (Ordonnance of St. Maxim of Trier) in October 1473 in favor of a division of the *ordonnance* company into four squadrons. Each of these squadrons was commanded by a *"chef d'escadre"* and consisted of 25 *lances*. Each squadron was made up of four *"chambres"* consisting of six *lances*.242

The infantry components and the mounted archers fought as individual units under the command of a *"capitaine"*. The various "branches" (e.g., crossbowmen or pikemen) formed *"centenies"* (centuries). These were each commanded by a *"centenier"* (centurion). The 300 mounted archers were divided into four *"escadrons"* (squadrons) when on the march. This organization of the army was more than complicated and Charles the Bold could seldom field so many archers and handgunners as was envisioned by the army regulations. The missing strength was made up with pikemen. In peacetime, only five *lance* leaders from a squadron were allowed to take leave at the same time along with 15 other soldiers; in wartime, it was two *lance* leaders and six additional soldiers at one time. The *ordonnance* companies each had a patron saint whose image was displayed on its banner.

As early as 1471, Charles attempted to raise twelve 900-man *ordonnance* companies, i.e., for a total of 10,800 men. Later, more *ordonnance* companies were raised. They varied greatly in their composition and strength, and it is only by exception that one can determine the exact strength at a specific point in time. For example, in June 1474 the Burgundian-Savoyard 18th Ordonnance Company, under Jean de Jaucourt, had a Burgundian half-company with 58 *"hommes d'armes"*243 and 231 archers and crossbowmen. The Savoyard part consisted of a squadron from the Waadtland (Vaud) under Sire de la Sarraz with 20 *"hommes d'armes"* and 25 crossbowmen, Antonio di Sallenova's squadron consisted of 20 *"hommes d'armes"* and 25 crossbowmen.244 Also other ordonnance companies were manned with soldiers from not only one nationality. For example, in June 1475, in the Count of Campobasso's 15th Ordonnance Company, essentially consisting of Neapolitans, there were 27 German *"couleuviers"*, i.e., hand-

---

237 See Michael and Embleton, p. 18–19.

238 See Ortenburg, Georg, *Waffen der Landsknechte, 1500–1650* (Augsburg: Weltbild/Bechtermünz 2002), p. 45.

239 See Walsh, *Charles the Bold and Italy*, p. 379.

240 From the french number *"dize"*, i.e. ten. See Heath, p. 41.

241 Both partial units, that with six *lances* and that with four *lances* were called *"chambres"* (singular *"chambre"*).

242 See Michael and Embleton, p. 12–13.

243 This term, which shows up in older descriptions, is confusing because it related to the (usually noble-born) *lance* leader, then to the armored horsemen who are also not designated as *"chevalier"*. The synonym *"gens d´armes"* is often used; the singular in both cases is called an *"homme d´armes"*.

244 See Witte, *Zur Geschichte der Burgunderkriege*, p. 45.

Crossbowman, shown from the *Veldenzer Aufgebot* (Veldenz Levy) reenactment group
Photo: Anja Hiebinger

Burgundian horsemen

gunners.[245] Although some of Europe's most heavily populated regions belonged to Charles the Bold's domains, he was unable to raise the needed numbers from his subordinates. Therefore, he hired Italian mercenaries to fill the ranks of his *ordonnance* companies. They were mostly war veterans and were not unjustly considered military specialists. That was especially the case for their commanders. Duke Charles was very keen on hiring the Venetian commander Bartolomeo Colleoni who had a larger than life reputation in Italy but was already over 70 years old. But the Venetians would not release Colleoni, claiming that they needed him themselves. The Duke of Burgundy's pay contracts usually had a three-year duration. That was a luxury that only rich Burgundy could afford. For example, on 10 November 1472, Charles engaged the Neapolitan Condottiere Cola di Monforte[246], Count of Campobasso, to perform three years of service along with 2,300 men. That number included 2,000 horsemen.[247] A large portion of Campobasso's troops, however, was not Italians, but Catalonians. In 1474 Duke Charles secured the services of Bartolomeo Colleoni and 2,500 men the latter hired, for three years, but again the Venetians did not play along. The Italian mercenaries went to war for the Duke of Burgundy under a different command.

The mercenary units' core forces, like for the Burgundian ordonnance companies, were the cavalry. Their armor was usually German or Italian models whereby the artful overlapping construction of the former allowed its wearer greater mobility than the more rigid Italian types. In the meantime, the armorer's art had reached its high point; the patterns were still Gothic. However, new style elements were emerging from Italy. The Ducal Court and Burgundian cavalry set the fashion elements for armor.[248] The armor offered almost all-round protection, while it still guaranteed the wearer a high degree of mobility. Often the pieces of armor for the left arm were made larger and stronger, which naturally was related to the requirements of fighting on horseback with a leveled lance.

Charles the Bold had armor manufactured by his court armorer Lancelot de Gindertale. The quality of this armor is said to have not been inferior to the models of famous Milanese master armorers.[249] There were many armorers' workshops in his domains, especially in Brussels where up to 73 master armorers worked. There were also such workshops in Ghent and Liège; however, in 1467 Duke Charles forbade the rebellious Liègoises from producing armor in the city.[250] A kind of mantle, called a *"manteline"* or *"journade"*, was worn over the armor after the Italian fashion. This piece of clothing had sleeves with slits and was often made of very expensive material like velvet or silk. It inspired the later *Landsknechte* in their costumes. Between 1461 and 1483 in France, the wearing of velvet and silk was forbidden in the ordonnance companies; the Burgundian cavalry were certainly more resplendent.[251] The helmets worn at that time were either closed visor-helmets or *Schaller* (with or without a visor that could be lowered). The *Schaller*, or sallet, was a streamlined type of helmet that was frequently used in England, the Neth-

---

245 See Paravicini, Werner, *Colleoni und Karl der Kühne* (Berlin: De Gruyter/Akademie, 2014), p. 85.

246 Actually "Nicola Pietravalle di Monforte".

247 See Walsh, Richard J., *Charles the Bold and Italy*, p. 346.

248 See Lanzardo, Dario (ed.), *Ritter-Rüstungen, Der Eiserne Gast, Ein mittelalterliches Phänomen* (Munich: Callwey, 1990, p. 61.

249 See Boeheim, Wendelin, *Handbuch der Waffenkunde*, p. 610.

250 See Michael and Embleton, *Armies of medieval Burgundy*, pp. 28–29.

251 See Funcken, Fred and Liliane, *Rüstungen und Kriegsgerät im Mittelalter*, Gütersloh : Prisma-Verlag, 1979), p. 36.

Pikemen and Handgunner
Photo: Susan Sümer

Soldiers
Photo: Susan Sümer

Burgundian cavalry, presented by *la IXe Companie d'Ordonnance* (9th Ordonnance Company) reenactment group
Photo: Anja Hiebinger

erlands and Burgundy. In Germany the *Schaller* was also worn very often, and ones produced there frequently had a long, extended neck protection in the rear. This type of helmet appears to have been developed in Italy; the German name *Schaller* and also the English designation "sallet" are derived from the Italian term "*celata*".

To supplement the *Schaller* there was also a protective device for the lower face and the throat, the so-called "*bavière*" (Old English: *beofor*, English: *bevor*, German: *Bart*). Because it was found to be a hindrance, it was often not worn. Charles the Bold's half-brother Cornelius died at the 6 June 1452 Battle of Rupelmonde when he was stabbed in the face by a pike while he was not wearing a "*bavière*". In the Battle of Montlhéry (on 16 July 1465), Charles himself received a laceration to his neck when his "*bavière*" fell down. Also, further developments of the war hat were worn, like the "*chapeau de Montauban*".[252]

A good, mass-produced set of armor for a 1.6 meter or 5 foot 3 inch tall fighter weighed about 25 kilograms or 55 pounds. A horse is capable of carrying about one quarter of its own weight of 350 to 500 kilograms or 770 to 1,100 pounds. A horseman's armor, helmet and weapons weighted about 30 kilos or 65 pounds, and the rider and saddle weighed a total of 80 kilos or 175 pounds, for a total of 110 kilos or 240 pounds, to which can possibly be added the weight of a horse's own armor. A "marshal" carried out the command of cavalry. Along with knights or knight-born squires ("*Edelknechten*"), there were also mounted men from the simple classes in the cavalry, who in Germany were called "*Reisige*". The previously mentioned mounted knife-fighters (*coutiliers*) as well as the light lancers were also considered as "*Reisige*". Mounted crossbowmen and later also handgunners were counted among them. Charles made use of the light cavalry for reconnaissance; especially among his Italian mercenaries there were some light cavalrymen. A round shield, still common in Italy, was one of their attributes.

The Burgundian army's archers were integrated into the ordonnance companies as mounted bowmen, who were often men from the Picardy, but also Englishmen were among them. The equipment of such archers included a bow, thirty arrows, a helmet, a sword and a dagger. That was set down in the duchy's statutes. They often wore boots made of soft leather that reached to the knees. Most of the English archers served in their own units. The English archers, like the city and town militiamen (the pikemen from Flanders in particular), were difficult to integrate into the *ordonnance* companies, so mostly archers from Picardy appeared. English archers, English mercenaries generally, entered Charles' service individu-

---

252 See Planché, James Robinson, *An Illustrated Dictionary of Historic Costume: From the First Century B.C. to C. 1760*, Vol. 1 (London, 1876) (Reprint: Mineola, New York: Dover, 2003), p. 89.

Soldier with armor and *"Schaller"* helmet
Photo: Susan Sümer

ally or as groups. Larger units were subordinated to him from the English crown based on the alliance. He took them on for the most part (after the English-Burgundian campaign) as mercenaries. In the early years of Charles' reign Englishmen were already the most sought-after mercenaries even though they were not very numerous at that time. During the 1467 campaign against Liège there were some, and in 1472 there were eleven English knights, 27 mounted archers and sixteen (foot) archers listed in the Burgundian army's records. In 1471, English King Edward had promised to provide considerably more soldiers. However, he took his time fulfilling his promise. But in 1473 he sent around 2,000 archers, in 1474 another 1,000 archers and 13 knights. In July 1473 the English distinguished themselves with the storming of Nijmegen's Nieuwstad-Tor (New City Gate), where they hoisted their banner. During the siege of Neuss they attracted the attention of observers. Afterward, Duke Charles took a portion of the Englishmen to form its own ordonnance company (with an organizational structure significantly deviating from the standard) under the command of Sir John Middleton, as an integral part of his army. After already being employed in the stalled Anglo-Burgundian campaign against France, 2,000 Englishmen joined the Duke of Burgundy's service.[253] He valued his English soldiers, paying the English archers higher wages than the others. Additionally, he took many into his Household's forces, the *"maison ducale"*. Thus, there were eight companies

---

[253] See Wadge, Richard, *Arrowstorm, The World of the Archer in the Hundred Years War* (Stroud: The History Press, 2007).

Burgundian soldiers
Photo: Susan Sümer

of English archers with a total of almost 800 men. A select troop of forty English archers served him as a personal bodyguard.[254]

The archers were armed with a yew longbow as tall as they were, with a pull-weight of about 100 pounds (or greater). In the hands of a practiced archer, it was a fearsome weapon. The English archers brought their equipment along from the island. Because the only English continental possession, namely the city and harbor of Calais, was completely surrounded by Burgundian territory, supply from England was not a problem. However, the best wood for bows at that time came from southern France and the Iberian Peninsula. The production of arrows was a somewhat less difficult undertaking. A huge number were needed so the choice of wood was less selective. In the 1465 Battle of Montlhéry, the Burgundian army's archers shot 38,400 arrows in one day.[255] The arrows could have hunting heads (broadheads) that were effective mostly against unarmored opponents, or various awl-shaped heads (bodkins) that were also effective against light armor. There were also arrowheads that could penetrate plate armor. Along with those, there were arrows with light field points (flights) that could be used for practicing[256] or for long distances. The English archers were sought after specialists in Burgundy, but also in England where the War of the Roses raged from 1455 to 1485. However, there were periods of relative quiet that allowed some archers to look around for new employment on the Continent. There the situation was different because the archers seldom had to deal with enemy members of their own profession. The famous archery duels that were so typical of the fighting in the War of the Roses could hardly be expected on the Continent.

The archers carried swords, daggers, and short clubs as sidearms and were equipped with open helmets or sallets with visors and light body armor (asketons or brigandines). In 1475, Duke Charles had 2,000 English archers in his army, while during the Battle of Nancy around 1,000 English archers in ten companies were present who were almost completely wiped out. A Captain John Turnbull[257] (according to his name, a Scot) brought only 34 men from his originally 97-man company back to their homeland.[258] Sir John Middleton fought his way through to the English possession of Calais with the remainder of his ordonnance company. Another field commander, Thomas Everingham from Yorkshire, with 100 archers fought at Crespin a month after the catastrophe at Nancy. The following year he and his 80 bowmen fought with a mostly Flemish unit that defeated the French at Izegem.

In the Battle of Guinegate on 7 August 1479 he served in the later Emperor Maximilian's army and commanded 500 (mostly English) archers. The morale and cohesion among the English were very high but Charles the Bold did not know how to employ them, i.e., adequately massed. Furthermore, he could have completely redefined the role of the nobles' cavalry, which he either was unable or did not want to do. Also, the footsoldiers (mainly pikemen) from the northern domains did not enjoy any priority with the Duke. They were used more as gap-fillers "*Lückenbüßer*", although they were very numerous. During the 1475 occupation of Lorraine he used around 8,000 men – of them 2,000 were from Flanders, 2,000 from Brabant, 1,300 from Artois, and 1,000 from Hainaut. But these soldiers were well equipped; they also wore the Duchy's colors of blue and white. Duke Charles also employed men from the Flemish Shooting Guilds – archers, crossbowmen and handgunners. At the siege of Neuss there were twenty archers from Lille and twenty archers, six crossbowmen and six "*couleuvriniers*"[259] from Douai in his army. Thirty archers and sixty crossbowmen came from Bruges.[260] The discipline supposedly left much to be desired, the infantry from the north showed little respect to the nobles according to the chroniclers. Charles had to use them to compensate for the losses at Murten, which initially succeeded. Then the continued guerilla warfare on many fronts necessitated his further tribute: one month before the Battle of Nancy when they took rolls, there were still 1,136 cavalry from the nobility, 1,788 mounted archers and 2,463 footsoldiers.

Before the Battle of Murten the Duke of Burgundy had many more "regular" troops available: 1,741 heavy noble cavalry (500 of them belonged to the Duke's Household), 4,062 mounted archers (of them 1,377 English and supposedly also some mounted crossbowmen) and 4,445 footsoldiers. Because Charles' army at Murten had been stronger and the difference had by no means been made up by the Savoyards, the portion of the feudal levies and the city and town militias made up a very large part of the Burgundian army. Later the feudal levy portion would be greater when the losses among the mercenaries had to be made up. Charles demanded that three soldiers had to

---

254 See Léderrey, Ernest, "*Les armées de Charles le Téméraire durant les guerres de Bourgogne*", in *Revue Militaire Suisse*, Vol. 107 (Lausanne, 1962), pp. 368–382, specifically p. 370.

255 See Michael and Embleton, *Armies of Medieval Burgundy*, p. 31.

256 They were the easiest to remove from practice targets.

257 In the Burgundian documents he is called "Tourneboulle". He was an experienced veteran. He had served in the English garrison in Calais in 1451/52, then he became a pirate for a short time, and in 1454 he captured a Dutch ship, before he entered Burgundian service.

258 See Turnbull, p. 180.

259 The 'shooters' armed with culverins ("*couleuvrines*"), i.e., light handguns.

260 See Crombie, Laura, "Defense, Honor and Community; The Military and Social Bonds of the Dukes of Burgundy and the Flemish Shooting Guilds", in Curry, Anne and Bell, Adrian R., *Journal of Medieval Military History*, Vol. IX (Woodbridge: Boydell and Brewer 2011), pp. 75–95, specifically pp. 84–85.

Burgundian handgunner
Photo: Anja Hiebinger

be provided for each fifty hearths of a town. At least one of the soldiers had to report into the army with a sword, dagger and glaive.[261]

Charles had learned of the value of archers in the 1452 Battle of Rupelmonde when the Picardy archers in the Burgundian Army (then still under Duke Philipp the Good) had exchanged volleys with Ghent's handgunners and won the upper hand.

Even though the archers were considered the pride of the Duke's army, the Duke was more taken with his artillery. Burgundy, with its foundries in High Burgundy and the Wallonia, had not only very advanced cannon material, but also very numerous cannon. In 1474 Charles had 780 artillerymen (among them 65 master cannon-makers, 49 carpenters and 544 engineers) who manned 133 cannon – supported by hundreds of drivers and peasants.[262] Later, the Duke strengthened his artillery further and placed many additional pieces in service. But they did not accomplish much in the Burgundian Wars – on the contrary, each time when the Swiss went up against the Burgundians the cannon became booty for the Swiss. Among the approximately 200 cannon captured at Murten and the 103 at Nancy, undoubtedly very many were of smaller calibers. For example, the "*crapadeaux*" small cannon were widely used in France and Burgundy.[263] Also the actually antiquated "*couleuvrines*" (culverins), served by two men and mounted on large forked supports or on wagons, were still on hand in great numbers.[264] At the beginning of the 15th century, "*couleuvrines*" were banded together and mounted on wheeled carriages. Such a cannon was called a "*ribauldequin*". They were employed to defend against enemy attacks. Aside from in Eastern Europe, their use was no longer common in the area dealt with here. But it is known that Burgundian artillerists employed such "*ribauldequins*" at the second Battle of St. Alban (on 17 February 1461) on the side of the House of York against the supports of the House of Lancaster.[265]

At Neuss, Charles the Bold fielded 17 large bombards, ten "courteaux" and 202 "serpentines", without being able to achieve any significant success. The Burgundians' most important type of cannon was the "serpentine", and the German term "*Feldschlange*" ("field snake or field serpent) is derived from it. This type of cannon first appears around 1430. Serpentines were smoothbore cannon with a seven to ten centimeter (2 ¾ to 4 inch) caliber. The barrels were mostly fire-fused iron staves, over which white-

---

261 See Boeheim, p. 343.
262 See Schmidt-Sinns, Dieter, *Studien zum Heerwesen der Herzöge von Burgund (1465–1479)* (Göttingen: (dissertation), 1967), p. 14.
263 See Smith, Robert Douglas and DeVries, Kelly, *Medieval Weapons: An Illustrated History of Their Impact* (Santa Barbara et al.: ABC CLIO 2007), p. 294.
264 These "*couleuvrines*" represented a larger variant of the "*couleuvrines á main*" (hand culverins).
265 See Ramsay, Syed, *Tools of War, History of Weapons in Early Modern Times* (New Delhi: Alpha Editions, 2016.

In the Italian mercenaries' camp
Photo: Susan Sümer

Borselen commanded the ships until 1474 and exercised important functions in the Burgundian court. He enjoyed a semiautonomous position, although he was a knight in the Order of the Golden Fleece, he was also an admiral in the French service. Henrik van Borselen died in 1474 and his son Wolfert became his successor in many important offices.

Charles the Bold attempted to give his army uniforms. Starting in 1471 they were supposed to wear "mi-parti" style tunics, blue on the right side and white on the left. That was laid down in the 31 July 1471 Abbeville Ordinance (*Ordonnance d'Abbeville*). The armored horsemen had blue and white plumes on their helmets. These colors were often worn laterally reversed, but also frequently not at all. More universal was the use of the Burgundian cross of St. Andrew, frequently in red, less often in yellow or blue. The Burgundians had used this insignia since 1416. The efforts to create a somewhat common appearance for the Burgundian army must not mislead one to think that this army lacked internal coherence: "the mechanisms/arrangements of the same, when seen from outside, were amazing and some, like the organization of the artillery, were highly meritorious, but the whole gigantic army lacked homogeneity and above all esprit de corps".[269]

The Burgundian army's tactics under Charles the Bold focused on using the artillery's and gunners' firepower. Charles tried to let the enemy attack his own front in order to expose them to the Burgundian's concentrated fire. Cavalry counterattacks were then to shatter the enemy. But this kind of operation was seldom used with success. Even when the Burgundian army remained in a strong defensive position and the enemy attacked, the latter could come away victorious like the Swiss and their allies at Murten. It was even more difficult for the Burgundians to attack the enemy when they did so from a movement. Charles used the feigned retreat by the advance guard as a tactic as his father had done in 1452 at Rupelmonde. However, Duke Philipp the Good had been successful then, while with Charles the same process ended in disaster at Grandson. It is difficult to recognize consistent tactical features in the Duke of Burgundy's campaigns. He experimented and copied the English and French tactics as well as the ancient examples. When deploying the Burgundian army units, the duke positioned the infantry, often reinforced by dismounted horsemen, in the center, and the cavalry on the flanks. He frequently had the field artillery move up in front of the infantry, for example at Nancy he employed 30 cannon in this manner that could have caused the Swiss serious losses if they had made a frontal attack. In 1473, Charles established that the cavalry should always maintain a close formation. The mounted archers should dismount to fight, their horses' reins should be fastened to the pages' saddles so the advancing archers' horses could be quickly brought after them. The pikemen should march in close order and in front of the archers. On the command from the archers' commander, the pikemen were to deploy crouched with their long pikes toward the enemy so the archers could shoot over them. The archers and the pikemen were also trained to form squares with the horses (of mounted bowmen) in the middle. From Commynes' writings it is known that the Burgundian army's archers used sharpened stakes as defensive obstacles completely following the English example. Charles concerned himself with many details regarding tactics, training and equipment. He admired the commanders of antiquity; Gobelin paintings with depictions of Hannibal and Alexander the Great hung in the great halls of his Brussels palace.[270] He had a translation prepared of Caesar's "*De Bello Gallico*". Undoubtedly, he emulated his role models of antiquity, but he certainly could not hold a candle to them. He was a stellar military organizer who personally settled detailed questions in numerous decrees. He recognized the problems of military logistics better than many of his contemporaries. But he was not a great field commander; he made poor decisions on the battlefield. He had outstanding reconnaissance capabilities in the light cavalry of his Italian mercenaries. He wantonly neglected them, frequently not giving their observations necessary importance. "On top of everything, Duke Charles failed not only in the most difficult leadership problem – recognizing the time when to give up formerly correct decisions, but also his stubbornness."[271]

That was not the case for the enemy.

---

269 Boeheim, p. 16.

270 See Parker, Geoffrey, *Cambridge illustrated History of Warfare* (Cambridge: Cambridge University Press, 1995, p. 105.

271 Fiedler, Siegfried, *Taktik und Strategie der Landsknechte, 1500–1650* (Augsburg: Bechtermünz, 2002), p. 200.

The Swiss and Their Allies

It is an untrue cliché that the Swiss were a people of peaceful farmers and shepherds who only went to war when their homeland was threatened. The Swiss, that is the Swiss Confederation and the residents of the associated "lieus" (German "*Orte*") also went to war outside their spheres of influence and they also did so even if alliance responsibilities were not the reason. They were actually always prepared for war. They practiced using weapons from childhood, although there was seldom any organized military training.[272] The principle of universal military obligation applied from the age of 14 (later from 16) to 60 years. The *Tagsatzung*, a kind of parliament of the representatives of the individual Confederation lieus (cantons), established the number of soldiers and then the cantonal leadership ordered the mobilization. That is how the Swiss armies' numerical superiority in that period can be explained. However, the Swiss often attacked when they had fewer men, even when the numerical ratios were clearly unfavorable (e.g., in 1444 against the Armagnacs).[273] Their absolute military readiness, great bravery and martial sense were the Swiss Confederation's hallmarks.[274] Thus, the simple soldier went to war with his weapon, aiming for a ruthless, aggressive effect. That was with a swinging halberd, sword, dagger and axe in both hands. Firearms were not widely used, but nevertheless played a certain role. Armor was not considered especially important, at least not initially. For the larger number of pikemen employed, protective gear was still necessary logically. The principle was that each Swiss soldier was to arrange for his own equipment, however, relative to his wealth. Poor men received what they needed for military service from the arsenal. If a soldier had debts, a creditor was not allowed to take away his weapons. If someone wanted to become a citizen in a Swiss Confederation city, he absolutely had to demonstrate he owned appropriate military equipment. The cantons' levies were subdivided in the *Auszug* ('move-out' – it mostly included the unmarried men between 16 and 30 years old), the *Landwehr* (militia – they were somewhat older) and the *Landsturm* who were only called up in the direst emergencies. The cantons with a large portion of urban inhabitants (like Zurich) organized the fighters from the city dwellers according to guilds.

Along with defensive wars against neighboring princes and also lesser rulers (and the constant fighting against the Swabian and Upper Alsatian knights that were already legendary there) the Swiss also undertook pillaging raids often enough. The wars the Swiss Confederates waged in the 15th century were usually ones of aggression. Then they were often the younger sons of alpine peasants who could not find adequate work at home. Even in times of war, bands of volunteers under their own captains marched along with the cantons' levies. The volunteers had to supply themselves but used the opportunity to plunder. In the Burgundian Wars the Swiss infantry showed itself to be basically changed and to have tremendous fighting power. The tactical formation was a mass (German "*Gewalthaufen*"), thirty to fifty men wide and equally deep. The outermost ranks were made up of experienced men who carried the 18 to 20 foot (5.5 to 6 meter) pike[275] and were equipped with a half suit of armor. In the middle of the formation were men with halberds (*Helmbarten* or *Hellebarden*), other polearms like bills (*Roßschindern*), glaives, voulges, guisarmes, Lucerne hammers (*Luzerner Hämmern*) and suchlike. The great strength of the Swiss lay it their formidable marching speed and their ability to immediately go over from marching order to the attack. The men armed with long pikes could stop enemy cavalry or drive back enemy foot troops, and then the halberd wielding men from the interior of the square emerged and attacked into the melee. In 1386 at Sempach the Swiss had already fought in a wedge-shaped attack formation called a "*Spitze*" (point). During the Appenzell Wars the Swiss deployed in elongated squares (with broader rather than deeper ranks). Then the pikemen stood on the flanks, later also in the front rows. From that developed the previously mentioned thirty to fifty-man wide and deep *Gewalthaufen* (mass). The pikemen in the foremost ranks had to be really fearless, physically strong and experienced fighters. For them, first contact with the enemy meant there was no going back because the rear ranks were pressing relentlessly forward. If the Swiss succeeded in penetrating the enemy formation, the battle was won. The Swiss held the long pike (whose shaft was slightly conical) at the balance point, i.e., about one third from the lower end. When the pikes were lowered, the points of the fourth rank protruded another half meter or 18 inches in front of the foremost rank.[276] The Swiss had painfully experienced the effect of the long pike at their defeat by the Milanese in 1422 at Arbedo and had promptly adopted it into their own arsenal where it gradually complemented and replaced the halberd.

Around 1400, about 80 percent of the Swiss footsoldiers were armed with the halberd, at Murten it was still 40 percent. A powerful thrust with this weapon could even penetrate plate armor cuirass. The Lucerne hammer ("*Luzerner Hammer*"), named after a mass archeological find near Lucerne, was very similar to the halberd, however with a hammer-like head instead of the axe edge, and it was apparently a Swiss specialty. Soldiers with such a weapon could be extremely dangerous to an armored horseman. Equally feared were the soldiers with the two-

---

272 See Schaufelberger, Walter, *Der alte Schweizer und sein Krieg* (Zurich: Europa, 1966), p. 43.

273 See Keegan, John, *Die Kultur des Krieges* (Berlin: Rowohl, 1995), p. 467.

274 See Fiedler, p. 30.

275 See Urban, William, *Medieval Mercenaries, The Business of War* (London: Boydell and Brewer, 2006), p. 217.

276 See Ortenburg, p. 45.

hander sword (German "*Zweihänder*"). They were mostly handpicked men who had proven their ability with the weapon with a fencing master. They received double pay and were often the commanders' bodyguards or the guards for the banners. Additionally, the Swiss sword and Swiss dagger, which differed in the blades' length and width, were in use.[277]

Horsemen did not play a big role for the Swiss, and only Bern had a "horse banner" ("*Rossbanner*") with 100 armored lancers and 200 mounted, lightly armed men. The other cantons each had a very small number of mounted crossbowmen for reconnaissance and courier duties.[278] When it occasionally states in literature that Swiss had employed cavalry in large numbers at Murten in 1476, then it is a misunderstanding. The horsemen came for the most part from the Lower Union or they were provided by the Habsburg's vassals (thought part of the territories were located in what is now Swiss territory).

---

277 See Messner, p. 113.

278 See Fiedler, p. 38.

Soldiers in clothing and armor typical of the period
Photo: Anja Hiebinger

The long-range weapons used by the Swiss footsoldiers were the crossbow and the handheld firearms. The latter were initially in the form of crude culverins. Then in the course of the 15th century smoothbore matchlock muskets spread from Italy. The longbow was only seldom used. The oldest verified use of handheld firearms by the Swiss was in 1385-86 at the siege of Rothenburg in the Sempach War. Around the middle of the 15th century the ratio of crossbowmen to handgunners was eight to one. It is certain that at the Battle of Nancy in 1477 there were about 800 Swiss handgunners present who were concentrated in the rearguard. Normally the Swiss "shooters" ("Schüt- zen") – the term did not differentiate between handgunners ("Feuerrohrschützen"), archers ("Bogenschützen") or crossbowmen ("Armbrustschützen") - operated as skirmishers and were concentrated in the advance guard.

The crossbowmen used the winch's gripping mechanism (or "cranequin"), which appeared at the time of the Burgundian Wars. At this time pavises were no longer used by Swiss crossbowmen. Artillery was not a hallmark for Swiss warfare. On one hand it did not fit into the Swiss military tradition because it would have strongly diminished their units' marching speed, and on the other hand the Swiss Confederation hardly had the possibility to produce cannon themselves. At the siege of Waldshut (July to August 1468) the Bernese shot in the city gate with their stone-firing cannon. But they had purchased this cannon in 1415 in Nuremberg. Then naturally the Burgundian spoils brought some and in part very advanced cannon that were expensive to produce into the Swiss arsenals.

Wagon laagers were not part of the Swiss standard tactical repertoire.[279] Their baggage train was comparatively small. They took fewer wagons along than did other contemporary armies. The Prince-Bishop of St. Gallen, as lord of one of the territories allied with the Swiss Confederation before the Battle of Grandson, offered 155 men. He paid extra for two pipers and two wagon-drivers. The latter had to service the large supply wagon ("*Reiswagen*"). On it were 170 arrows (crossbow bolts?), two barrels, two large field cauldrons with chains and hooks, eight bowls, and a *Viertel* of salt and more than two *Malter* of toasted oats.[280] The Swiss carried along provisions on their military campaigns, but the Confederation troops often pillaged. Even in allied territories the Swiss fighters frequently pillaged. For example, after the Battle of Nancy during their march home, the Swiss passed through Mülhausen and plundered the Jews there. "They ruthlessly helped themselves to whatever they wanted, on their own initiative commandeered wagons and horses, stole like ravens and tormented the population."[281] If there was something that demoralized the Swiss, then it was hunger. Therefore, their campaigns had to be concluded quickly; the Swiss "always had accomplished what they planned within eight days or lost".[282]

Pay and booty were not infrequently the decisive motivation for a Swiss soldier to go to the field. It is no coincident that the term "*Reisläufer*", which originally was nothing but a man who fought on foot (as opposed to a mounted "*Reisigen*"), was applied to a mercenary. Swiss men sought military service with foreign employers even when there was a threat of sanctions at home. If their own people performing foreign military service endangered the homeland's policies, then sometimes the authorities imposed fines (like in the case of a mercenary who fought against the Abbot of Kempten in 1460) or banishment for life. Even a death penalty could be imposed.

The prohibition against taking prisoners that was imposed during the Burgundian Wars and was later renewed, was intended to maintain the Swiss contingents' coherence and discipline. Some military operations occasionally went astray when individual soldiers or groups trying to take captives interrupted them. The Swiss military successes were if nothing else a result of obedience and trust in the military leader, who was successful again and again in converting impetuous aggressiveness and lust for booty into militarily sensible operations. Among the commanders were often representatives of the nobility, e.g., the most famous knight serving as a Swiss commander being Adrian von Bubenberg from Bern, the hero of Murten. Indeed, these personalities mostly fought on foot like the simple Swiss soldiers, but they rode on the march. Therefore, they wore armor that was not dissimilar to that of the Burgundians. The commanders and standard-bearers proudly wore berets (usually red) decorated with feathers. These feathers or plumes were frequently in the canton's colors: white-blue-white for Zug, red-white for Unterwalden, yellow-brown-yellow for Uri and blue-white for Lucerne, just to name a couple examples. The Swiss relationship to knighthood was basically ambivalent. When before the Battle of Murten some campaign participants were dubbed knights, it did not significantly delay the allied army's attack, but it also caused resentment among the simple Swiss soldiers. The Bernese seem to have placed greater store in a knight's title than did people from Lucerne. When three men from Lucerne were to be dubbed knights, two of them in a row refrained from accepting the honor. [283]

In this period, the Swiss did not produce any distinguished command personalities. The Swiss army's complex command structure reflected the political structure of the Confederation. The individual cantons' contingents were commanded by their own captains who also often occupied political functions in the Swiss cantons. Decisions were made by the council of war, which was a very effective arrangement for the Swiss. Having two army wings separate but directed to attack a common objective was a very effective tactic. So a frontal and a flank attack could be simultaneously executed. This tactic, which was used very effectively at Héricourt and Nancy, naturally required an exact knowledge of the terrain.

The Swiss went to the Burgundian Wars under the flags of their home cantons. However, the exception was the Battle of Nancy where the Swiss fought as mercenaries for the Duke of Lorraine. It is notable that even the flagstaffs were kept in the colors of the cantons. (See illustration on pages 50-51 and 53 for examples of cantonal flags).

The Swiss mastered marching in lockstep, which is characteristic for modern armies, or at least contemporary depictions show that. To do this, acoustic signals were of great importance. Therefore, each infantry formation had a drummer and a fifer.

---

279 See Rodt, Emanuel von, *Geschichte des Bernerischen Kriegswesens, Von der Gründung der Stadt bis zur Staatsumwälzung von 1798* (Bern: C. A. Jenni, 1831), p. 199.

280 For "*Viertel*" and "*Malter*" see footnotes 144 and 145 above.

281 Fiedler, p. 44.

282 Ochsenbein, p. 346.

283 See Furrer, Norbert et al. (Ed.), *Gente ferocissima: Solddienst und Gesellschaft in der Schweiz (15.-19. Jahrhundert)* (Zurich: Schweizerische Zeitschrift für Geschichte/Revue suisse d'histoire / Rivista storica svizzera, 1987), p. 187.

Firing a light fieldpiece
Photo: Anja Hiebinger

The Swiss contingents' large 'war horns' ("*Harsthörner*") fell into a different category.[284] They were a hallmark like the Scottish highlanders' bagpipes in later centuries. Their sounds were audible at a great distance and their psychological effect on friend and foe must have been tremendous. They gave the signal to attack. In the cases of Uri and Lucerne, they were actually huge horns, supposedly from aurochs.[285] For the other cantons they were "real" brass wind instruments.

Bilstein Castle
Photo: Christian Amet

Foraging on the march was very important for the Swiss armies' campaigns. The frequently repeated prohibition against taking prisoners shows that despite all the uncompromising by the Swiss military leadership, it still happened often enough. A prisoner of high rank held the promise of a ransom. After the victorious Battle of Héricourt, the prisoners were valued as follows: for a captured knight one could demand 1,600 guilders, for an armored cavalryman (but not even knight-born) 50 guilders, and 33 simple solders should bring in 198 guilders.[286] A young boy had no ransom value, so he was simply given to Wilhelm Herter. One could hope for a huge ransom for a prisoner of high rank and name. For example, at the Battle of Nancy, Count Engelbert II of Nassau and Vianden, an important Burgundian army commander and confidante of the Duke of Burgundy, became the captive of the knight Hans Marx von Eckwersheim who had fought with the Strassburg contingent.[287] The latter and a couple friends could not resist the attempt and kept the prize for themselves. As a result, the Strassburgers stormed the knight's castle (Burg Bilstein). Count Engelbert remained under arrest in Strassburg for a few months, until he could raise the 50,000 guilder ransom.[288] With it the Strassburgers were able to cover a part of their wartime costs (the Burgundian Wars had cost them approximately 165,000 guilders).

The Swiss Confederation's Alsatian, Swabian and Lorraine allies were an important addition in that they compensated for the weaknesses of the Swiss army. The cavalry and artillery were mostly provided by the allies. Furthermore, they could solve an annoying problem for the Swiss: Swiss Army contingents and leaders often competed, analogous to the competition of their home cantons, most especially between Bern and Zurich. Sometimes it was much quicker to agree to a non-Swiss man as the overall commander.

In the Holy Roman Empire the old feudal army system continued to exist until well into the 14th century, especially in the east. In the west, and also in Alsace, the French model was taking over more strongly. The cavalry's elite was sometimes – but falsely – referred to as "*Renner*" ('runners') and that is an indication that the knights' military function and the social status were diverging from one another. The "*Glefe*" (glaive) unit was normally somewhat smaller then the French "*lance*". Along with the knight, it was made up of an armored knife-fighter ("*Degenkämpfer*") comparable to the "*coutilier*", a light cavalryman or mounted crossbowman, and the "*Renner*'s" page.[289] But the system varied very widely. So in the Empire up to ten fighters made up a *Glefe*, but the number was most often less, sometimes it was just three fighters.

The city or town unions ("*Städtebünde*") that were common throughout the Empire – the Lower Union was also originally one of these – hired elite cavalry units. The knights' unions ("*Ritterbünde*") grew up on the model and were already common in southwestern Germany.

Also in the German regions, the commander of a military unit did not necessarily have to be a knight. In 1421 when the territories in Alsace sent their levy of 57 *Glefen* (glaives) to the Imperial Army for employment against the Hussites, the Mülhausen contingent was under the command of the 'squire' ("*Edelknecht*") Lud-

---

284 A *Harsthorn*, *Harschhorn* or *Harschhorn* was a signal horn made to imitate a bull's horn. Source: www.enzyklo.de/Begriff/Harschhorn

285 The aurochs also known as urus or ure (Bos primigenius), is an extinct species of large wild cattle that inhabited Europe,

286 See Rochholz, p. 126.

287 See Ehm-Schnocks, p. 146.

288 See Strobel, Adam Walther, *Vaterländische Geschichte des Elsasses von der frühesten bis auf die gegenwärtige Zeit, Dritter Teil* (Strassburg: Schmidt und Grucker, 1843), p. 362.

289 See Nicolle, David, *Medieval Warfare Source Book, Warfare in Western Christendom* (London: Arms & Armour, 1999), p. 170.

Fully armored Soldier at the time of the Burgundian War, shown by the *Veldenzer Aufgebot* (Veldenz Levy)
Photo: Anja Hiebinger

wig Meyer von Hüningen. In the sources, knights usually appear as (Latin) "*milites*", the squires ("*Edelknechte*") as "*armiger*", the "*Reisigen*" (mounted soldiers) often as "*écuyer*", sometimes also as "*Renner*".

The wealthier citizens from Strassburg, Basel, Colmar and more Alsatian towns served as cavalrymen. In Strassburg there was even a multi-branched city nobility, which in part owned considerable properties in the surrounding areas. The nobles' cavalry, which was organized in "*Glefen*", made up a considerable part of the city's military strength. Frequently, hired mercenaries were added to the cavalry. As late as the end of the 14th century, "*Freischaren*"[290] played a substantial role in the Alsatian towns' military strength, and they were called "*Blutharste*". But back to the cavalry as a branch. Its nucleus was still the armored knight and squire. Around the middle of the 15th century, a mounted soldier received a monthly payment of a Rhenish guilder, footsoldiers received half of that as a rule.

Princes of the Empire relied on noble's cavalry for their campaigns and they often recruited them from the knights' unions ("*Ritterbünde*").

A marshal commanded the cavalry. This position was as a rule hereditary, highly respected and also one that was associated with a not inconsiderable income. The Counts von Pappenheim were the hereditary marshals of the Empire during this timeframe. As a rule, when someone accepted an office in a prince's court, it came with the obligation to provide the prince with "*Reisige*", i.e., equipped cavalrymen. Along with persons actually in positions at court, the prince's counselors, tax collectors, *Rentmeisters* and *Forstmeisters* had to provide equipped mounted soldiers and horses.

The cities' and towns' infantry was organized based on guilds and crafts. The city/town militias were structured by quarters of the urbanization in order to effectively defend a section of wall and gates. Each quarter was under a "*Viertelmeister*" (literally a 'quarter master') appointed by the council. This *Viertelmeister* sometimes also had civil responsibilities like firefighting and supervision of the marketplace. Often the *Viertelmeister* was also the "*Bannerträger*" (in the sense of a "*Bannerherr*" – the standard bearer leading the quarter's troops). Then in Switzerland he was called a "*Venner*". He was supported by other officers, semi-professional gatekeepers, trumpeters and starting the end of the 14th century a "*Büchsenmeister*" ('master of the guns or culverins'). There were some examples for militia-like units for the rural population. The most famous example was the "*Hauensteiner Landfahnen*" (Land Flag of Hauenstein) from the southern Black Forest that belonged to the Habsburg's forelands. However, that troop was supposedly poorly equipped and armed (only with halberds). The designations for the footsoldiers varies widely in the sources: "*Trabanten*", "*Buben*", "*Pöck*" or "*Pöcke*", later also "*Landsknechte*" (the term "*Landsknechte*" first appears in writing in the Prussian chronicle by Johann von Posilge at the beginning of the 15th century).

For the most part the Swiss allies' footsoldiers came from the city and town levies. Even the artisans and merchants from the cities and towns considered the Burgundians and especially the Duke of Burgundy as hostile, and the cities were the actual opponents of Charles the Bold's claims to power. The city and town levies were deeply rooted in urban society, even though they often lapsed into having to hire mercenaries (many Swiss among them). The urban levies' weapons were stored in the city or town arsenals. For example, the oldest passed down inventory from the Basel arsenal from 1414 showed 324 crossbows (along with 6,000 bolts), 68 culverins and 17 cannon.[291]

The Swiss judged the military value of the allies' footsoldiers very critically. In November 1476, they expressed the wish that the cities of Strassburg, Colmar and Schlettstadt should send money as their contribution instead of footsoldiers because "they would not be useable" for the war – (Swiss German "*ze der were nit verfanklich*"). The footsoldiers from Basel on the other hand were welcome because the City of Basel has good people" ("*aber die statt Basel haby guot lüt*" in Swiss German).[292]

More important than the Allies' footsoldiers were their cannon. When Blamont was besieged in early summer, the Allies brought three large cannon into use: of the three "*Hauptbüchsen*" (large cannon), the "*Kätherlein*" came from Alsatian Ensisheim, the "*Metze*" from Bern, and a large "*Tarrasbüchse*"[293] from Basel that was named "Rüde". But only after the giant cannon from Strassburg, called the "Strauss", was brought there were they able to force the Blamont garrison to capitulate. It is not possible to determine what kind of cannon Strassburg's "Strauss" was. It supposedly weighed 55 "*Zentner*" (ca. 2,750 kilos or 3 tons). These bombards, when they were made with the stave-band process, fired along with "*Hagel*" (hail, i.e., scrap metal or canister) only stone balls because the resulting gas pressure buildup when firing iron balls

---

290 *Freischaren* (singular *Freischar*) were military units that were established without permission of or even against the wishes of authorities and set up for wartime undertakings. They originated either spontaneously – often based on gatherings (*Fasnacht*, church consecrations) - or were organized by individuals. The sources speak of "*Blutharsten*", "*Freiharsten*", "*Freiheiten*". The *Freischar* campaigns have to be distinguised from feuds and domestic unrest; they are related to the operations of the "*freien Reisläufer*" (serving in foreign lands). Source: *Historisches Lexikon der Schweiz*, http://www.hls-dhs-dss.ch/textes/d/D24629.php

291 See Hill, Jens and Freiberg, Jonas, *Krieger, Waffen und Rüstungen im Mittelalter, 800–1500* (Herne: VS-Books, 2013), p. 91.

292 Quoted from Wackernagel, p. 87.

293 A "*Tarrasbüchse*" (from the French terrasse, meaning an earthen bank or bastion) was essentially a siege cannon, according to Oelsner, Th., *Rübezahl: Der Schlesischen Provinzialblätter*, 9. Folge (Bresalu: F. Gebhardi, 1869), p. 81. An alternative derivation is that the "terrace" referred to the wooden platform on which it rested.

18th Ordonnance Company Flag
Photo: Anja Hiebinger

would inevitably cause the barrel to explode. The large siege cannon were almost exclusively "*Legstücke*" ("laying piece") that is cannon that were transported on special wagons but which had to be fired from a fixed platform with an end trestle beam or something similar.

Besides the Allies' heavy cannon the know-how of some allied commanders was of special importance. Many artillery officers had once been in the Burgundian service and knew not only the Burgundian army organization but also the idiosyncrasies of the Duke of Burgundy. Wilhelm Herter was one such person as was Friedrich Kappler.

Turning to Allied officers, peacock feathers on a beret were an insignia for officials, vassals or also supporters of the Habsburgs, by no means a traditional ally of the Swiss. Even the Upper Alsatian nobility were completely suspect for the Swiss, for centuries these proud knights had fought on the side of the Habsburgs against the Confederation and carried on some local feuds against them and their allies. The cities and towns in Alsace, the Sundgau and Swabia were more welcome as allies by the Swiss cantons. There were old friendships (e.g., between Zurich and Strassburg), and the cities of the region could often rely on the Confederation's help when they had feuds with the neighboring nobles. And again, it was the nobility of the forelands who were mistrusted in the Burgundian Wars. When, after the Burgundians' seizure of Lorraine, the Alsatians feared that Duke Charles could also attack their region, they began to take defensive measures everywhere. They thought of the example of Neuss and wanted to be ready to fight. Count von Thierstein, as the Habsburg's Governor, put the entire Sundgau on a defense alert. He sent his wife, Ottilia, to Mülhausen, considered safe, as a precautionary measure. The citizens of Ensisheim, his residence, took this very badly and did not send his household's belongings after his wife (as Thierstein had planned), but kept the goods for themselves.

THE "HENS' WAR" (*HENNENKRIEG*)

It is noteworthy that at the same time as the Swiss in alliance with Duke Sigismund of Tyrol were fighting against the Burgundians, Tyrolean princely stewards (*Landpflegern*) picked a fight in the name of (also maybe on behalf of) the Duke against close allies of the Swiss Confederation.

In 1464, Ulrich IX, Count of Matsch sold the castle and domain of Tarasp in the Unterengadin to Duke Sigismund of Tyrol for 2,000 guilders. Very quickly a conflict developed between the Duke and the Engadiners over the Tarasp Castle. The Bishop of Chur was summoned as a negotiator. In 1465, before negotiations could even begin, the Engadiners attacked the castle. However, the garrison was able to repulse the attack. In the beginning of May 1467, Duke Sigismund with troops from Vinschgau entered the Münster Valley and threatened all of Engadin from there, whereupon the Engadiners called upon the City of Chur and the Bishop for help. Thanks to negotiations by Count Nikolaus von Zollern, the parties came to an agreement on 23 May 1467. Reciprocal free trade was secured by the so-called "*Schludernser Richtung*" (the "Direction of Schluderns"). There was a clause in the treaty that obligated the Engadiners to provide the Duke 200 equipped footsoldiers for two months every year, who were to fight in the Duke's service without pay but for provisions and lodging (but not against the men of the League of God's House ("*Gotteshausleute*").[294] The following year Duke Sigismund ordered the *Landpflegern* (burggraves or stewards) and captains from each jurisdiction to send two or three men to Nauders as reinforcements. That was possibly a precautionary measure against the Engadiners. It is not clear whether it was related to the Bishop of Chur's conflict with the members of the League of the God's House who had occupied the Tschanüff Castle in Unterengadin. In Vinschgau the League of God's House members were so enraged at the prince's stewards of Nauders and Mals that they invited Count Georg (Jörg) von Werdenberg-Sargens to attack Mals and Nauders with them.

During the time when the Matsch family ruled them, the Unterengadiners had enjoyed some freedoms that the Habsburgs were not willing to grant them. As serfs or bondsmen they had to pay the landowners a tax, which entitled them to represent their peasants in foreign jurisdictions. This tax was paid in the form of hens, and due just before the beginning of Lent. The cause for the conflict was that in 1471 the Imperial judicial court in Glurns had taken away the "high jurisdiction" over Unterengadin from the Bishop of Chur (at this time Ortlieb von Brandis). Tyrolean and Bishopric domains geographically alternated close to one another there and the Bishop's subjects enjoyed greater freedoms. The Unterengadin court district had joined with other court districts, the City of Chur, the Bishopric Ministerials and the Cathedral Chapter of the League of God's House, that were all politically oriented against the Habsburgs' expansion efforts. The Bishop of Chur was trying to have good relations with Duke Sigismund of Tyrol. While he unwillingly accepted the arbitration verdict from Glurns, the people in Unterengadin were not ready to do so.

The "blood jurisdiction" ("*Blutgerichtsbarkeit*")[295] over Unterengadin lay with a judge who was the Duke of Tyrol's ministerial official or pledge lord (*Pfandinhaber*). This judge resided in the Naudersberg Castle. This situation displeased the Engadiners very much. In 1475, they refused to pay the official on the Naudersberg the tax in hens that was due in the Lenten period. For more than two years the Tyroleans and Engadiners fought one another over the issue in the resulting conflict, known as the "*Hennenkrieg*" – "Hens' War". The Tyrolean side began with an attack. Konrad Klamer, the *Pfleger* (Steward) of Nauders, and Captain Roland von Schlanersberg moved into Unterengadin for the campaign. The Tyroleans burned down the Tschanüff Castle in Engadin. Meanwhile the able-bodied men from the towns of Schleins and Remüs (now Ramosch) gathered on the mountains above the castle. Reinforcements from Oberengadin were also already on the way.

In a contemporary poem it said that the Tyrolean army commander, named Martinhans von Nauders, called to the captain of Engadiners, Wilhelm Gebhard (or "Bart Guglielm" in the local Romansh language), who had run into them at Remüs, that he should take off if he valued his life. The Engadiner answered that he would absolutely be willing to lose his life if he would gain honor in doing so. Then he ran his lance through Martinhans, broke into the eleventh rank of the Tyrolean army formation where he tore the flag from its staff before he sank down dead. That was the signal for the Engadiners' general attack, who then attacked from all sides. The Tyroleans fell back, or at least so says the legendary tradition.

The Naudersberg Castle was also battered. It was stormed and set afire. Duke Sigismund of Tyrol wanted to advance into the Engadin with a large army, however that did not happen. In 1477, a peace treaty, the "Peace of Fürstenau" ("*Friede zu Fürstenau*"), was concluded by negotiations between the Bishops of Brixen and Trient. Prisoners were exchanged and pillaged property was returned.

---

294 The "*Gotteshauseleute*", were members of the "*Gotteshausbund*", League of God's House, so-called from the Church of Coire, the head and capital of this league. The League of God's House was more or less a corporation of territorial estates with the bishop of Chur as its territorial lord. See Murray, John (ed.), *A Handbook for Travellers in Switzerland, the Alps of Savoy and Part of Dauphiné*, Vol. 2 (London: John Murray, 1886), p. 245; and Blickle, Peter and Dunlap, Thomas (translator), *Communal Reformation: The Quest for Salvation in Sixteenth-Century Germany* (Boston: Humanities Press, 1992), p. 34.

295 "In the Middle Ages, in the Holy Roman Empire, the blood jurisdiction, also known as *ius gladii*, right of the sword, blood spell, supreme judgment, civic jurisdiction, or custody of the county, was the embarrassing jurisdiction over crimes that could be punished with mutilations or with death". Source: https://educalingo.com/en/dic-de/blutgerichtsbarkeit

BURGUNDIAN "ORDONNANCE" COMPANIES
(in German: *"Ordonnanzkompanie"*)

The Duke's Guard, raised as the first "Ordonnance Companie"
Patron Saint: St. George
Commander: Olivier de la Marche

1st *Ordonnance Company*, raised in 1471 in the Netherlands (primarily in Flanders)
Patron Saint: St. Sebastian
Commander: Jacques de Harchies (from Hainaut/Hennegau, Belgium)

2nd *Ordonnance Company*, raised in 1471 in the Netherlands (primarily in Flanders)
Patron Saint: St. Adrian
Commander: Jean de la Vieiville (from Artois) until 1475, then Jean de Dammartin

3rd *Ordonnance Company*, raised in Burgundy in 1471
Patron Saint: St. Christopher
Commander: Jacques de Montmartin

4th *Ordonnance Company*, raised in 1472 in Savoy
Patron Saint: St. Antonius (Anthony)
Commander: Giacomo dei Vischi, Count of San Martino Canavese[296] I (from the Piedmont)

5th Ordonnance Company, raised 1472 in the Netherlands
Patron Saint: St. Nikolaus
Commander: Philippe Dubois, then Bernhard von Ravenstein[297], and then Jan van Broechhuisen (from Guelders)

6th Ordonnance Company, raised in 1472 in Burgundy
Patron Saint: St. John the Baptist
Commander: Gilles de Harchies (from Hainaut/Hennegau)

7th Ordonnance Company, raised in Burgundy in 1472
Patron Saint: St. Martin
Commander: Jacques de Rebrennes until 1475, then Philippe de Berghes

8th Ordonnance Company, raised in Burgundy in 1472
Patron Saint: St. Hubertus
Commander: Claude de Dammartin

9th Ordonnance Company, raised in the mortgaged lands (*Pfandlanden*) in 1472
Patron Saint: St. Catherine
Commander: Peter von Hagenbach, then Jean d'Igny, and then Antonio di Sallenova

10th Ordonnance Company, raised in Burgundy in 1472
Patron Saint: St. Julius
Commander: Baudouin de Lannoy (jun.), then Giacomo Galeotto

11th Ordonnance Company, raised in Burgundy in 1472
Patron Saint: St. Margaret
Commander: Amedée de Rabutin, then Ferry de Cusance, and then Georges de Menthon

12th Ordonnance Company, raised in Burgundy in 1472
Patron Saint: St. Avoye
Commander: Philippe de Poitiers, then Jean de Longueval, then Tommaso da Capua (an Italian Condottiere)

13th Ordonnance Company, raised in Burgundy in 1473
Patron Saint: St. Andrew
Commander: Josse de Lalaing, then Amedeo di Valperga (from the Piedmont)

14th Ordonnance Company, raised in Burgundy in 1473
Patron Saint: St. Stephen
Commander: W. de Soissons, then Louis de Soissons, and then Philippe de Loyette

15th Ordonnance Company, raised in the Netherlands in 1474, disbanded after the siege of Neuss
Commander: Louis de Berlaymont (from Hainaut/Hennegau)

15th Ordonnance Company (new creation), raised in Italy, primarily in Naples
Patron Saint: St. Peter
Commander: Cola di Monforte, Count of Campobasso

16th Ordonnance Company, raised in Italy in 1474
Patron Saint: St. Anne
Commander: Troylo de Muro da Rossano

17th Ordonnance Company, raised in Burgundy in 1474
Patron Saint: St. Jacob
Commander: Jean de Dommarien, then Louis de Montmartin

18th Ordonnance Company, raised in Savoy in 1474 (a half company of Burgundians, a half company of Savoyards)
Patron Saint: St. Magdalena
Commander: Jean de Jaucourt, Sire de Villarnoux, and then Humbert de Luyrieux

19th Ordonnance Company, raised in 1475
Patron Saint: St. Hieronymus
Commander: Dom Denys de Portugal

20th Ordonnance Company, raised from English mercenaries in 1475
Patron Saint: St. Lawrence
Commander: Sir John Middleton

21st Ordonnance Company, raised in Italy in 1475
Commander: Ruggerone d'Accrocciamuro, Count of Celano

22nd Ordonnance Company, raised in Italy in 1475
Commander: Pietro dei Corradi di Lignana, then Guglielmo dei Corradi Lignana (from the Piedmont)

---
296 In the Burgundian sources he is called "Jacques de Visque". In the Italian sources he shows up as "Jacopo dei Vischi".

297 He was killed during the siege of Neuss.

23rd Ordonnance Company, raised in Italy
Commander: Antonio dei Corradi di Lignana

24th Ordonnance Company, raised in Italy in 1476
Commander: Lodovico Taglianti d'Ivrea (from the Piedmont, he was the nephew of Giacomo dei Vischi)

25th Ordonnance Company, raised in Flanders in 1476
Commander: Josse de Halluin

26th Ordonnance Company, raised in Italy in 1476
Commander: D. Mariano

Some Companies, like the 19th or the 20th, were organized very differently from the standard *Ordonnance* Company.

(See McGill, Pat; Pacou, Armand and Riddell, Rod Erskine, *The Burgundian Army of Charles the Bold - The Ordonnance Companies and their Captains* (Lincoln: Freezywater Publications, 2001)

BIBLIOGRAPHY

Bennet, Matthew and Hooper, Nicholas, *The Cambridge Illustrated Atlas of Warfare: The Middle Ages, 768-1487* (Cambridge: Synopsis, 1996).

Blockmanns, William and Prevenier, Walter, *The Promised Lands: The Low Countries Under Burgundian Rule, 1369-1530* (Philadelphia: University of Pennsylvania Press, 1999).

Boeheim, Wendelin, *Handbuch der Waffenkunde, Das Waffenwesen in seiner historischen Entwicklung von Beginn des Mittelalters bis zum Ende des 18. Jahrhunderts* (Leipzig: Seemann, 1890).

Bömmels, Nicolaus, *Die Neusser unter dem Druck der Belagerung*, in *Neuss, Burgund und das Reich* (Schriftenreihe des Stadtarchivs Neuss, Bd. 6) (Neuss: Stadtarchivs, 1975).

Boersch, M. Charles, *Revue d'Alsace* (Strassburg: Bureau de la Revue D'Alsace, 1836).

Boué, Gilles, "Grandson and Morat" in Sandler, Stanley, *Ground warfare, An International Encyclopedia, Vol. 1* (Santa Barbara etc.: ABC CLIO, 2003).

Brauer-Gramm, Hildburg, *Der Landvogt Peter von Hagenbach, Die burgundische Herrschaft am Oberrhein 1469-1474* (Goettingen: Musterschmidt-Verlag, 2001).

Calmette, Joseph, *Die großen Herzöge von Burgund* (Munich: Diederichs, 1996).

Carey, Brian Todd, *Warfare in the Medieval World* (Barnsley: Pen and Sword, 2006).

Charles, Victoria, *Art of War* (New York, 2010).

Clayton, Anthony: *Warfare in Woods and Forests* (Bloomington and Indianapolis: Indiana University Press, 2012).

Clauss, Martin: *Ritter und Raufbolde. Vom Krieg im Mittelalter* (Darmstadt: Primus, 2009).

Commynes, Philippe de, *Memoiren* (Stuttgart: Kröner, 1972), a reprinting of *Les Memoirs de Messire Philippe de Commynes, Seigneur d'Argenton*.

Crombie, Laura, "Defense, Honor and Community: The Military and Social Bonds of the Dukes of Burgundy and the Flemish Shooting Guilds", in Curry, Anne and Bell. Adrian R., *Journal of Medieval Military History*, Vol. IX (Woodbridge: Boydell and Brewer, 2011), pp. 75-95.

Crowe, Eyre Evans, *The History of France*, Vol. 1 (London: Longman, Brown, Green, Longmans, and Roberts, 1830).

Daguet, Alexandre, *Geschichte der schweizerischen Eidgenossenschaft von den ältesten Zeiten bis 1866* (Aarau: H. R. Sauerländer, 1867).

Daniels, Emil, *Geschichte des Kriegswesens* (Leipzig: G.J. Göschen'sche Verlagshandlung, 1910).

Davies, Norman, *Verschwundene Reiche, Die Geschichte des vergessenen Europa* (Darmstadt: Konrad Theiss, 2013 - published in English as Vanished Kingdoms: The History of Half-Forgotten Europe: (London: Penguin, 2012).

Delbruck, Hans, *Geschichte der Kriegskunst im Rahmen der politischen Geschichte*, Teil 3 (Berlin: Georg Stilke, 1923).

Deuchler, Florens, *Die Burgunderbeute, Inventar der Beutestucke aus den Schlachten von Grandson, Murten und Nancy, 1476/1477* (Bern: Stämpfli, 1963).

DeVries, Kelly and Smith, Robert Douglas, *Medieval Military Technology* (Toronto: University of Toronto Press, 2012.

Domke, Helmut, *Flandern - Das burgundische Erbe* (Munich: Prestel, 1972).

Drake, Michael S., *Problematics of Military Power: Government, Discipline and the Subject of Violence* (London: Taylor & Francis, 2002).

Dubois, Henri, *Charles le Téméraire* (Fayard: Fayard le Grand Livre du Mois, 2004).

Duby, Georges, *Histoire de la France, Dynasties et revolutions de 1348 a 1852* (Paris: Larousse, 1987).

Duerrenmatt, Peter: *Schweizer Geschichte* (Zurich: Schweizer Druck- und Verlagshaus, 1963).

Ebel, J.G., *Anleitung auf die nützlichste und genussvollste Art die Schweitz zu bereisen*, 3. Teil (Zurich: Orell, Gessner, Füssli & Compagnie, 1810).

Ehlers, Joachim, *Geschichte Frankreichs im Mittelalter* (Darmstadt: Primus, 2009).

Ehlers, Joachim, *Die Ritter: Geschichte und Kultur* (Munich: C. H. Beck Wissen, 2006).

Ehm-Schnocks, Petra, *Burgund und das Reich: Spätmittelalterliche Außenpolitik am Beispiel der Regierung Karls des Kühnen (1465–1477)* (Munich: Oldenbourg, 2002).

Elgger, Carl von, *Kriegswesen und Kriegskunst der schweizerischen Eidgenossen im XIV., XV. und XVI. Jahrhundert* (Luzern: Militärisches Verlagsbureau, 1873).

Embleton, Gerry and Howe, John, *Söldnerleben im Mittelalter* (Stuttgart: Paul Pietsch Verlag, 1996) (Published in English as *The Medieval Soldier: 15th Century Campaign Life Recreated in Colour Photographs,* London: Windrow & Greene, 1994).

Fatio, Guillaume, *Au tour de lac Léman* (Geneva: Institut Polygraphique, 1902) (reprinted by Rother Verlag, Oberhaching, 1981).

Feller, Richard, *Geschichte Berns* (Bern: Lang, 1949).

Fiedler, Siegfried, *Taktik und Strategie der Landsknechte, 1500-1650* (Augsburg: Bechtermünz, 2002).

Fischer, Rudolf von, *Schweizer Kriegsgeschichte, Heft 2, Die Feldzüge der Eidgenossen diesseits der Alpen vom Laupenstreit bis zum Schwabenkrieg* (Bern: 1915).

Fowler, Kenneth, *Medieval Mercenaries, Volume I* (Oxford: Blackwell, 2001).

Frey, Emil, *Die Kriegstaten der Schweizer dem Volk erzählt* (Neuenburg: F. Zahn, 1904).

Fuchs, Ildephons, *Die mailändischen Feldzüge der Schweizer* (St. Gallen, 1810).

Funcken, Fred and Liliane, *Rüstungen und Kriegsgerät im Mittelalter* (Gütersloh : Prisma-Verlag, 1979).

Fuhrer, Hans Rudolf, *Militärgeschichte zum Anfassen; Dokumentation: Die Burgunderkriege* (Au, Zurich: 1999).

Furrer, Norbert et al. (Ed.), *Gente ferocissima: Solddienst und Gesellschaft in der Schweiz (15.-19. Jahrhundert)* (Zurich: Schweizerische Zeitschrift für Geschichte/Revue suisse d'histoire/Rivista storica svizzera, 1987).

Furrer, Sigismund, *Geschichte von Wallis*, Band 1 (Sion: Calpini & Albertazzi, 1850).

Gaier, Claude, *Art et organization militaires dans la principauté de Liège et dans le comté de Looz au Moyen âge* (Brussels: Académie Royale de Belgique, 1968).

Geiger, Benjamin, *Die Burgunderkriege, Die Schlachten von Grandson und Murten 1476, in Pallasch Zeitschrift für Militärgeschichte*, No. 43 (Salzburg: Österreichischer Milizverlag, 2012).

Gravett, Christopher and McBride, Angus, *German Medieval Armies, 1300-1500* (London: Osprey, 1998, Men-at-Arms Series No. 166).

Hampe, Theodor, *Die fahrenden Leute in der deutschen Vergangenheit* (University of Michigan reprint of the 1902 original edition (Leipzig: Eugen Diederichs) (Norderstedt: BoD – Books on Demand, 2014).

Hansjakob, Heinrich, *Der Waldshuter Krieg vom Jahre 1468* (Waldshut: Heinrich Zimmermann, 1866).

Hay, Denys, *Europe in the Fourteenth and Fifteenth Centuries* (London: Routledge, 1989).

Heath, Ian, *Armies of the Middle Ages*, Volume 1 (Worthing: Wargames Research Group, 1982).

Heller, Kevin Jon and Simpson, Gerry (Ed.), *The Hidden Histories of War Crime Trials* (Oxford: Oxford University Press, 2013).

Henne, Josef Anton, *Schweizerchronik in vier Buechern, Drittes Buch* (St. Gallen: Büreau des Freimütigen, 1834).

Hill, Jens and Freiberg, Jonas, *Krieger, Waffen und Ruestungen im Mittelalter, 800-1500* (Herne: VS-Books, 2013).

Historischer Verein in St. Gallen (Ed), *Neuiahnsblatt* (St. Gallen, 1861).

Hormayr, Joseph von, *Taschenbuch für vaterländische Geschichte*, Band I (Leipzig: Georg Franz, 1837).

Keegan, John, *Die Kultur des Krieges* (Berlin: Rowohl, 1995) (Published in English as *A History of Warfare* (New York: Random House, 1993)).

Kekewich, Margaret L., *The Good King, René of Anjou and Fifteenth Century Europe* (Basingstoke: Palgrave Macmillan, 2008), p. 239.

Kendall, Paul Murray, *Louis XI: the Universal Spider* (New York: W. W. Norton, 1970).

Kleiman, Irit Ruth, *Phlippe de Commynes, Memory Betrayal, Text* (Toronto: University of Toronto Press, 2013).

King, Andy, "Gunners, Aides and Archers", in: Curry Anne and Bell, Adrian R., *Journal of Medieval Military History* Vol. IX (Woodbridge 2011), pp. 65-75.

Kirk, John Forster, *History of Charles the Bold, Duke of Burgundy*, Vol. III (London: J. Murray, 1868).

Koch, H.W, *Medieval Warfare* (London: Crescent, 1978).

Köllner, Friedrich, *Geschichte des vormaligen Nassau-Sarbrück'schen Landes und seiner Regenten,* 1. Band (Saarbrücken: Heinrich Arnold, 1841)

Kroll, Stefan and Krüger, Kersten (Ed.), *Militär und ländliche Gesellschaft in der frühen Neuzeit* (Hamburg: LIT Verlag, 2000).

Kurz, Hans Rudolf: *Schweizerschlachten* (Bern: Francke, 1977).

Lange, Joseph, "*Pulchra Nussia. Die Belagerung der Stadt Neuss durch Herzog Karl den Kühnen von Burgund 1474/75*", in: *Neuss, Burgund und das Reich (Schriftenreihe des Stadtarchivs Neuss, Bd. 6)* (Neuss: Stadtarchiv, 1975), p. 28f.

La Société Générale d'Histoire Suisse (Ed.), *Indicateur d'HIstoire Suisse* (Solothurn 1877).

Lanzardo, Dario (Ed.), *Ritter-Rüstungen, Der Eiserne Gast, Ein mittelalterliches Phänomen* (Munich: Callwey, 1990).

Léderrey, Ernest, "*Les armées de Charles le Téméraire durant les guerres de Bourgogne*», in *Revue Militaire Suisse*, Vol. 107 (Lausanne, 1962), pp. 368-382.

Lienert, Meinrad, *Schweizer Sagen und Heldengeschichten* (Stuttgart: Levy & Müller, 1915).

Liliencron, Rochus von (Ed.), *Die historischen Volkslieder der Deutschen*, Band 2 (Leipzig: Vogel, 1866).

Löhrer, Friedrich J., *Geschichte der Stadt Neuss von Ihrer Gründung an bis jetzt* (Neuss: Druck und Verlag E. Schwann, 1840).

McGill, Pat; Pacou, Armand and Riddell, Rod Erskine, *The Burgundian Army of Charles the Bold - The Ordonnance Companies and their Captains* (Lincoln: Freezywater Publications, 2001).

Meier, Werner, "*Eidgenössischer Solddienst*", in: Kroll, Stefan and Krüger, Kersten (Ed.): *Militär- und ländliche Gesellschaft in der frühen Neuzeit*, Hamburg 2000.

Messner Florian; Ollesch, Detlef; Seehase, Hagen and Vaucher, Thomas, *Der Engadiner Krieg: Eine Reise in die Renaissance* (Eltville: RWM Bureau, 2016).

Metsdorf, Jens, "*Bedrängnis, Angst und große Mühsal*" – *Die Belagerung von Neuss durch Karl den Kühnen 1474/75*, in: "*…würfen hin in steine/grôze und niht kleine… Belagerungen und Belagerungsanlagen im Mittelalter*" (Beihefte zur Mediaevistik, Bd. 7) (Frankfurt a. M.: Olaf Wagener, 2006).

Meyer, Werner and Lessing, Erich, *Deutsche Ritter, deutsche Burgen* (Munich: Orbis, 1976).

Michael, Nicholas and Embleton, Gerry, *Armies of Medieval Burgundy, 1364-1477* (London: Osprey, 1983, Men-at-Arms Series, 144).

Miller, Douglas and Embleton, Gerry, *The Swiss at War, 1300-1500* (London: Osprey, 1979, Men-at-Arms Series, 94).

Mohr, Conradin von, *Geschichte von Currätien und der Republik "„gemeiner drei Bünde"* (Chur: Verlag der Antiquariats-Buchhandlung, 1870).

Mone, F.J. (Ed.), *Zeitschrift fuer die Geschichte des Oberrheins*, Band 6 (Karlsruhe: Braun'schen, 1855).

Monter, William E., *A Bewitched Duchy, Lorraine and its Dukes 1477-1736* (Geneva: 2007), p. 23.

Müller, Johannes von, *Die Geschichten Schweizerischer Eidgenossenschaft* (Reutlingen: J. J. Mäcken'schen Buchhandlung, 1825.

Nicolle, David, *Medieval Warfare Source Book: Warfare in Western Christendom* (London: Arms & Armour, 1999).

Nüscheler, David, *Geschichte des Schweizerlandes*, Band 2 (Schaffhausen: Hurter'schen Buchhandlung, 1847).

Oakeshott, Ewart, *European Weapons and Armour: From the Renaissance to the Industrial Revolution* (Woodbridge: Boydell and Brewer, 1980).

Ochs, Peter, *Gechichte der Stadt und Landschaft Basel*, Band 4 (Basel: Schweighauser'schen Buchhandlung, 1819).

Ochsenbein, Gottlieb Friedrich, *Die Urkunden der Belagerung und Schlacht von Murten* (Freiburg: Bielmann, 1876).

Ortenburg, Georg, *Waffen der Landsknechte, 1500-1650* (Augsburg: Weltbild/Bechtermünz, 2002).

Paravicini, Werner, *Guy de Brimeu, Der burgundische Staat und seine adlige Führungsschicht unter Karl dem Kühnen* (Bonn: Ludwig Röhrscheid, 1975).

Paravicini, Werner, *Karl der Kühne, Das Ende des Hauses Burgund* (Göttingen: Muster-Schmidt 1976).

Paravicini, Werner, *Colleoni und Karl der Kühne* (Berlin: De Gruyter/Akademie, 2014).

Parker, Geoffrey, *Cambridge Illustrated History of Warfare* (Cambridge: Cambridge University Press, 1995).

Payne-Gallwey, Sir Ralph, *The Book of the Crossbow* (Reprint: New York: Dover, 1995).

Pfister, Christoph, *Die alten Eidgenossen: Die Entstehung der Schwyzer Eidgenossenschaft im Lichte der Geschichtskritik und die Rolle Berns* (Norderstedt: Paul Haupt, 2013).

Pfister, Johann Christian von, *Geschichte von Schwaben, Neu untersucht und dargestellt*, 2. Buch, 2. Abteilung (Stuttgart: Daniel Class, 1827).

Planché, James Robinson, *An Illustrated Dictionary of Historic Costume: From the First Century B.C. to c. 1760*, Vol. 1 (London: 1876) (Reprint: Mineola, New York: Dover, 2003).

Ramsay, Syed, *Tools of War, History of Weapons in Early Modern Times* (New Delhi: Alpha Editions, 2016).

Reid, William, *Buch der Waffen, Von der Steinzeit bis zur Gegenwart* (Dusseldorf and Vienna: Econ, 1979).

Remy, Andreas, "*Descriptions of Battles in Fifteenth Century Urban Chronicles*", in Curry, Anne and Bell, Adrian R., *Journal of Medieval Military History*, Vol. IX (Woodbridge: Boydell and Brewer, 2011), pp. 118-131.

Rochholz, Ernst Ludwig (ed.), *Eidgenössische Liederchronik* (Bern: C. Fischer, 1842).

Rodt, Emanuel von, *Geschichte des Bernerischen Kriegswesens, Von der Gründung der Stadt bis zur Staatsumwälzung von 1798* (Bern: C. A. Jenni, 1831).

Rodt, Emanuel von, *Die Kriege Karls des Kühnen, Herzogs von Burgund und seiner Erben* (Schaffhausen: Hurter'sche Buchhandlung, 1844).

Rodt, Emanuel von, *Karl der Kühne* (Bern: Hallwag, 1941) (first published in Schaffhausen in 1843).

Rütz, Dieter, "Die Reiterei der Eidgenossen", in: *Die Zinnfigur*, Ausgabe (Issue) 4, 2017, p.107.

Sandler, Stanley, *Ground Warfare, An International Encyclopedia*, Vol. 1 (Santa Barbara etc: ABC-CLIO, 2003).

Schaufelberger, Walter, *Der alte Schweizer und sein Krieg* (Zurich: Europa, 1966).

Schaufelberger, Walter, *Der alte Schweizer und sein Krieg, Studien zur Kriegsführung vornehmlich im 15. Jahrhundert* (Frauenfeld: Huber, 1987).

Schelle, Klaus, *Karl der Kühne, Burgund zwischen Lilienbanner und Reichsadler* (Stuttgart-Degerloch: Seewald, 1977).

Schmidt-Sinns, Dieter, *Studien zum Heerwesen der Herzöge von Burgund (1465-1479)* (Göttingen: (dissertation), 1967).

Schneider, Emil, *Geschichte der Stadt Mülhausen im Elsass* (Mülhausen: J. Brinkmann, 1888).

Seehase, Hagen and Krekeler, Ralf, *Der gefiederte Tod, Die Geschichte des Englischen Langbogens in den Kriegen des Mittelalters* (Ludwigshafen: A. Hörnig, 2001).

Seehase, Hagen and Ollesch, Detlef, *Kurfürst Friedrich der Siegreiche von der Pfalz (1425-1476)* (Petersberg: Imhof Verlag, 2013).

Seldner, Heinrich, *Lüttich, die zweite burgundische Dynastie und die Markgrafen Karl und Markus von Baden, 1455-1468* (Rastatt: Grossherzoglich Museum, 1865).

Shaw, Christne, *Barons and Castellans, The Military Nobility of Renaissance Italy* (Leiden and Boston: Brill, 2015).

Smith, Robert Douglas and Devries, Kelly, *The Artillery of the Dukes of Burgundy, 1363-1477* (Woodbridge: Boydell Press, 2005).

Smith, Robert Douglas and DeVries, Kelly, *Medieval Weapons: An Illustrated History of Their Impact* (Santa Barbara etc.: ABC CLIO, 2007).

Sporschil, Johann, *Die Schweizer-Chronik, Von der Stiftung des Rütli-Bundes bis zum ewigen Frieden mit Frankreich* (Leipzig: Kayser, 1840).

Strobel, Adam Walther, *Vaterländische Geschichte des Elsasses von der frühesten bis auf die gegenwärtige Zeit, Dritter Teil* (Strassburg: Verlag Schmidt und Grucker, 1843).

Stierlin, Rudolf Emanuel, *Die Burgundischen Kriege* (Bern: Huber und Comp. Körder und Fehr, 1840).

Tillier, Anton von, *Geschichte des eidgenössischen Freistaates Bern*, Band 2 (Bern: Chr. Fischer, 1838).

Tobler, Gustav, *Conrad Pfettisheims Gedicht ueber die Burgunderkriege* (Bern: K. J. Wyss Erben, 1917).

Tumbull, Stephen, *The Book of the Medieval Knight* (London: Crown, 1985).

Ulrich, Adolf, *Akten zum Neusser Kriege 1472-1475*, in *Annalen der historischen Vereins* för den Niederrhein, No. 49 (Hannover: Hofdruckerei der Gebrüder Jänecke, 1889).

Urban, William, *Medieval Mercenaries, The Business of War* (London: Greenhill Books, 2006).

Vaughan, Richard, *Charles the Bold, The Last Valois Duke of Burgundy* (London and New York: Boydell Press, 1973).

Vulpinus, Theodor, *Ritter Friedrich Kappler, Ein Elsässischer Feldhauptmann aus dem 15. Jahrhundert* (Strassburg: Ed. Heitz, 1896).

Wackernagel, Rudolf, *Geschichte der Stadt Basel. Zweiten Bandes erster Teil* (Basel: Helbing & Lichtenhahn, 1911).

Wadge, Richard, *Arrowstorm, The World of the Archer in the Hundred Years War* (Stroud: The History Press, 2007).

Wälchli, Karl F., *Adrian von Bubenberg* (Bern: Haupt, 1979).

Wagner, E., Drobna, Z. and Durdik, J., *Medieval Costume, Armour and Weapons* (London: Andrew Dakers, 1962).

Walsh, Richard J., *Charles the Bold and Italy, Politics and Personal* (Liverpool: Liverpool University Press, 2005).

Walter, Bastian, "Urban Espionage and Counterespionage during the Burgundian Wars (1468-1477)", in: Curry, Anne and Bell, Adrian R.: *Journal of Medieval Military History Vol. IX* (Woodbridge: Boydell and Brewer, 2011), p. 132-145.

Wieland, Johannes, *Geschichte der Kriegsbegebenheiten in Helvetlen und Rhätien als Handbuch zum Militärunterricht für Schweizeroffiziere aller Waffen,* Band 1 (Basel: Schweighauser'schen Buchhandlung, 1827).

Wierstraet, Christian, *Die Geschichte der Belagerung von Neuss, Faksimile der Erstausgabe bei Arnold their Hoernen, Köln 1476. Übertragung und Einleitung Herbert Kolb* (a facsimile of the first edition by Arnold ther Hoernen published in Cologne in 1476, translation and introduction by Herbert Kolb) (Neuss: Galerie Küppers, 1974).

Wilson, John, *History of Switzerland* (London: Longman, Rees, Orme, Brown, Green, & Longman, 1832).

Witte, Heinrich, "Zur Geschichte der Burgunderkriege", in: *Zeitschrift für die Geschichte des Oberrheins* (Freiburg im Breisgau: Kohlhammer, 1891), pp. 2-81.

Würdinger, Josef, *Kriegsgeschichte von Bayern, Franken, Pfalz und Schwaben,* Erster Band (Munich: Literarisch-Artistische Anst. der Cotta'schen Buchhandlung, 1868).

Zellweger, Johann Caspar, *Geschichte des Appenzellischen Volkes* (Trogen: Meyer und Zuberbühler, 1834).

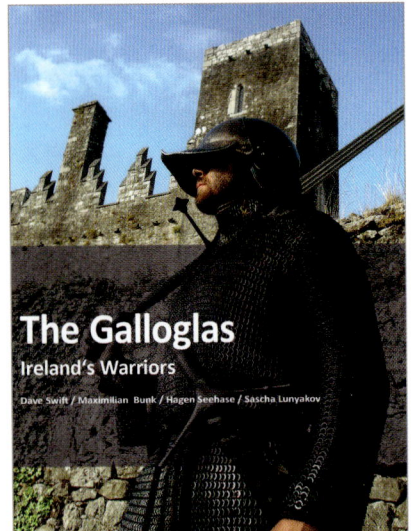

Dave Swift / Maximilian Bunk / Hagen Seehase

The Galloglas
From the Western Isles to Ireland

From their appearance in the 13th century to the 16th century wars of the Tudor age, the so-called galloglas determined the manner in which war was waged on Irish soil. While traditional Irish warfare mainly relied on swift-footed hit-and-run tactics, these battle-hardened warriors stood and fought it out to the last man, galloglass often facing galloglass. The era of the galloglas reached its gory climax in the Battle of Knockdoe in 1504. Described as huge, violent and raw-boned by contemporary sources, these warriors represented an archetypical element of Irish warfare, and yet they had their origins in the Hebrides off the Scottish coast. This book seeks to describe the origins, the history and the eventual disappearance of the galloglas from the battlefields of Ireland. Drawing on the latest archaeological evidence, it sheds light on the outward appearance, weapons and equipment, pay, organisation, and the motivation of these fearsome warriors. The book was written in cooperation with Claíomh, one of the leading Irish reenactment groups reconstructing the daily life of the galloglas. Apart from numerous photographs of reenactors in reconstructed galloglas equipment, this volume contains detailed photographs of weapons and equipment as well as of historic locations, contemporary illustrations, and specially commissioned artwork.
Paperback, 115 mostly color illustrations, two maps, english text. 156 pages.
ISBN 978-3-96360-063-0

Florian Messner / Hagen Seehase

Venetian War of 1487
... or the War of Rovereto

The 1487 Venetian War between the maritime, major power Venice and the alpine Archduchy of Tirol began from insignificant events and led to considerable political disruptions - especially in Tirol. The conflict is closely tied to Archduke Sigismund of Tirol's partially tragic, partially odd biography. The Venetian War occurred on the threshold between the ending Middle Ages and the beginning of modern times: on one side the knightly duel between Johann von Waldburg-Sonnenberg und Antonia Maria da Sanseverino, and on the other the drawn-out battle with heavy artillery for the city and castle of Rovereto. The Battle of Calliano was decisive: on one side, a veteran of the Burgundian Wars, on the other a highly respected condottiere, with the breathtaking mountains of the Adige Valley as the backdrop. For the first time, the new type of soldier, the Landsknecht was decisive in battle. The material remains of the Venetian War are partially still visible today and a scientific treasure trove for archaeologists and historians. This book came about in close cooperation with reenactment groups from Italy, Austria and Germany. It contains, along with detailed depictions of weapons, color illustrations and some excellent reconstruction drawings by Wolfgang Braun.
Paperback, one map, 41 photos, partly of re-enactment events, nine contemporary images, two b / w drawings, two double-page color drawings by Sascha Lunyakov. 100 pages
ISBN 978-3-96360-027-2

Alexander Querengässer / Sascha Lunyakov

Hussite Warfare
The Armies, Equipment, Tactics and Campaigns 1419-1437

With the outbreak of the Hussite Revolution in 1419, Bohemia found itself opposed by a superior force of European crusader armies. German knighthood was experiencing its last heyday. But the Bohemian heretics' army, under the leadership of energetic commanders like Jan Ziska, developed tactics with which they won one battle after another. The employment of the defensive Wagenburg ("wagon castle") and intensive use of the first cannon as field artillery brought them many successes. The Hussites were the first soldiers since Roman times to employ all the available branches in coordination on the battlefield. This book highlights not just the history of the conflicts, but also the weapons and military branches, organization and tactics of the Hussite armies.
Paperback, 64 moustly colour illustrations, 10 maps,
18 color plates by Sascha Lunyakov. 144 pages.
ISBN 978-3-96360-017-3

**Ask your bookseller or
have a look at the well-known online retailers.**